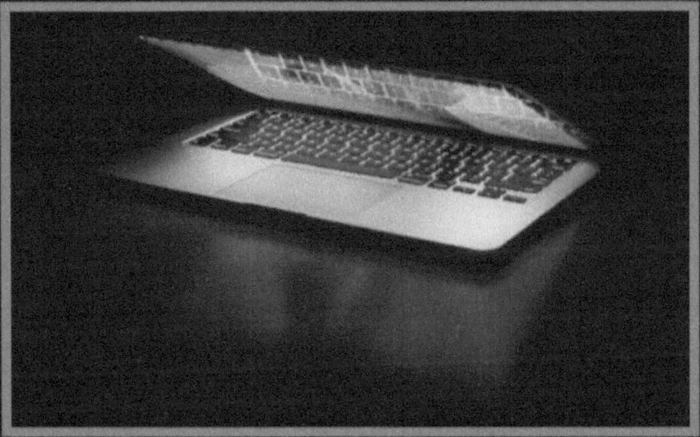

Serverless Machine Learning
and Artificial Intelligence

Get hands-on experience with practical examples and step-by-step guides to build your own serverless AI application.

Katie Millie

Serverless Machine Learning and Artificial Intelligence

Get hands-on experience with practical examples and step-by-step guides to build your own serverless AI application.

By

Katie Millie

Copyright notice

Copyright © 2024 Katie Millie. All Rights Reserved.

Welcome to the enchanting realm of Katie Millie, where the fusion of creativity and innovation crafts mesmerizing experiences. Every piece of content on this site, encompassing text, images, graphics, and designs, is the sole property of Katie Millie and is safeguarded by international copyright laws. Any unauthorized use, reproduction, or distribution of this material without explicit written consent from Katie Millie is strictly forbidden.

Immerse yourself in the exquisite artistry and meticulous craftsmanship that characterize Katie Millie, appreciating that each creation is a reflection of unparalleled originality and superior quality. By exploring this site, you commit to respecting the intellectual property rights and recognize the dedication and talent that have brought this content to fruition.

We sincerely thank you for your understanding and support in maintaining the integrity and distinctiveness of Katie Millie's artistic endeavors.

Table of Contents

INTRODUCTION

Chapter 1

    The Allure of Artificial Intelligence

        The Traditional AI Struggle: The Server Monster

            Enter the Serverless Savior: Unleashing AI with Ease

Chapter 2

    The Power of Serverless Computing for AI

        The Pay-as-You-Go Advantage: Serverless Machine Learning and Artificial Intelligence

            Scaling Without the Stress: Serverless Machine Learning and Artificial Intelligence

                Serverless vs. Traditional AI Development: A Game Changer

                    Who Benefits from Serverless AI? (Spoiler Alert: Everyone!)

Chapter 3

    Top Cloud Platforms for Serverless AI Development

        Google Cloud Functions: A Flexible Option for Serverless ML and AI

            Azure Functions: Building AI on Microsoft's Cloud

                Choosing the Right Platform for Your Serverless ML and AI Needs

Chapter 4

    Serverless Frameworks: Simplifying Development (e.g., Serverless Framework, AWS SAM)

Machine Learning Frameworks in the Serverless World (e.g., TensorFlow, PyTorch)

Model Deployment and Management Services (e.g., Amazon SageMaker, Google AI Platform)

Integrating with APIs and Data Sources: Building the AI Ecosystem

Chapter 5

Hands-On with Serverless AI: A Step-by-Step Guide

Designing Your Serverless AI Architecture: Breaking Down the Workflow

Coding Your Serverless AI Hero: Putting the Pieces Together

Deploying Your AI Application: Unleashing Your Serverless Masterpiece

Chapter 6

Common Serverless AI Use Cases and Applications

Chatbots and Virtual Assistants: Powering Intelligent Conversations

Fraud Detection: Keeping Your Business Safe from Bad Actors

Predictive Analytics: Foreseeing the Future with AI Insights

Chapter 7

Training and Managing Your Serverless AI Models

Model Versioning and Control: Keeping Track of Your AI Evolution

Monitoring and Debugging Your Serverless AI Applications

Chapter 8

Serverless Batch Processing: Handling Large

Datasets with Ease
　　　　　Optimizing Performance and Cost Efficiency
　　　　　　　Security Considerations for Serverless AI Applications
Chapter 9
　　　Emerging Trends and Advancements in Serverless Technologies
　　　　　The Ethical Implications of AI and Serverless Development
Chapter 10
　　　Your Journey to Serverless AI Mastery: The Final Call to Action
　　　Appendix
　　　Glossary of Key Terms

INTRODUCTION

Serverless Machine Learning and Artificial Intelligence: Unleash the Power of AI Without Becoming a Server Superhero

Imagine a world where artificial intelligence (AI) isn't a mythical beast locked away in server farms, but a readily available tool you can wield with ease. A world where building intelligent applications doesn't require wrestling with complex infrastructure, but feels more like snapping together Lego bricks. That world, my friend, is the future of serverless machine learning.

This book isn't your typical, dry AI manual. We're not going to delve into the nitty-gritty of server maintenance (unless you crave nightmares). Instead, we're here to unveil the magic of serverless, a revolutionary approach to AI that lets you focus on the "what" and "why" of your intelligent applications, leaving the "how" to the cloud.

Why Serverless? Why Now?

The world is hungry for AI solutions. From fraud detection to medical diagnosis, AI is transforming industries at a breakneck pace. But the traditional path to AI is riddled with roadblocks. Provisioning servers, managing configurations, and scaling infrastructure – these tasks are time-consuming, expensive, and frankly, a major pain point.

Serverless computing throws a lifeline to aspiring AI heroes. It allows you to build and deploy intelligent applications without the burden of server management. You simply upload your code, and the cloud takes care of the rest. It's like having a team of invisible server ninjas working tirelessly behind the scenes, ensuring your AI application runs smoothly and scales seamlessly.

The Captivating Catch of Serverless AI

But the benefits of serverless AI extend far beyond convenience. Here are just a few reasons why you should be jumping on the serverless bandwagon:

- **Cost-Effectiveness:** You only pay for the resources your AI application uses. No more idle servers draining your budget. Serverless is a pay-as-you-go playground for AI experimentation.
- **Scalability on Autopilot:** Need to handle a sudden surge in traffic? Serverless scales automatically, ensuring your AI application is always available, no matter the demand.
- **Faster Time to Market:** Forget months spent on infrastructure setup. Serverless lets you deploy your AI application in a flash, giving you a competitive edge in the ever-evolving world of technology.
- **Focus on Innovation:** With server management out of the picture, you can dedicate your time and energy to the truly exciting part – building innovative AI solutions that make a real difference.

This Book: Your Guide to Serverless AI Mastery

This book is your comprehensive map to the exciting territory of serverless machine learning and artificial intelligence. We'll equip you with the knowledge and tools you need to navigate this landscape with confidence. Whether you're a seasoned developer or an AI enthusiast dipping your toes into the waters, this book caters to all levels.

Here's what you can expect:

- **Demystifying Serverless:** We'll break down the core concepts of serverless computing and how it applies to AI development.
- **The Serverless AI Toolkit:** We'll explore the leading cloud platforms and tools that empower you to build and deploy serverless AI applications.
- **Building Your First Serverless AI Hero:** Get hands-on experience with practical examples and step-by-step guides to build your own serverless AI application.
- **Beyond the Basics:** We'll delve into advanced topics like model training, deployment strategies, and monitoring your serverless AI applications.

By the end of this journey, you'll be well on your way to becoming a serverless AI champion. You'll have the skills to leverage the power of AI without getting bogged down in server complexities. So, are you ready to unleash the potential of AI with the magic of serverless? Let's dive in!

Chapter 1

The Allure of Artificial Intelligence

Artificial Intelligence (AI) has captured the imagination of individuals and industries alike, offering a glimpse into a future where machines can learn, reason, and make decisions. The allure of AI lies in its potential to revolutionize various sectors, from healthcare and finance to entertainment and transportation. With advancements in serverless computing and the integration of machine learning (ML) and AI capabilities, harnessing the power of AI has become more accessible and scalable than ever before.

The Promise of AI

AI's appeal stems from its ability to process vast amounts of data, identify patterns, and make predictions with remarkable accuracy. This ability translates into numerous practical applications:

- **Healthcare**: AI can analyze medical images to detect diseases like cancer at an early stage, assist in drug discovery, and personalize treatment plans based on individual patient data.

- **Finance**: AI algorithms can detect fraudulent transactions, predict market trends, and provide personalized financial advice.

- **Transportation**: Autonomous vehicles use AI to navigate and make real-time decisions, enhancing safety and efficiency.

- **Entertainment**: AI powers recommendation systems for streaming services, creating personalized user experiences.

Serverless Machine Learning and AI

Serverless computing, where the cloud provider dynamically manages the allocation of machine resources, has emerged as a powerful paradigm for deploying AI and ML applications. Serverless architectures, such as Azure Functions, enable developers to run code without provisioning or managing servers. This approach offers several benefits:

- **Scalability**: Serverless platforms automatically scale to handle varying loads, ensuring that applications remain responsive even during peak usage.

- **Cost Efficiency:** With serverless computing, you only pay for the computer time you use, making it cost-effective for sporadic or unpredictable workloads.

- **Simplified Management:** Developers can focus on writing code and developing models rather than managing infrastructure.

Building AI Applications with Azure Functions

Azure Functions, a serverless compute service from Microsoft Azure, provides an excellent platform for deploying AI and ML models. By integrating with other Azure services, developers can build robust, scalable AI applications. Here, we'll explore a simple example of deploying an ML model using Azure Functions.

Example: Deploying a Machine Learning Model

Suppose we have trained a machine learning model to predict housing prices based on various features like location, size, and number of bedrooms. We can deploy this model using Azure Functions and make predictions via an HTTP endpoint.

1. Train the Model: First, we train a simple ML model using Python and scikit-learn.

```python
from sklearn.datasets import load_boston
from sklearn.model_selection import train_test_split
from sklearn.linear_model import LinearRegression
import joblib

# Load dataset
boston = load_boston()
X = boston.data
y = boston.target

# Split data
X_train, X_test, y_train, y_test = train_test_split(X, y, test_size=0.2, random_state=42)

# Train model
model = LinearRegression()
model.fit(X_train, y_train)

# Save model
joblib.dump(model, 'housing_model.pkl')
```

2. Create Azure Function: Next, we create an Azure Function to load the model and make predictions.

```python
```

```python
import logging
import joblib
import json
import numpy as np
from azure.functions import HttpRequest, HttpResponse

def main(req: HttpRequest) -> HttpResponse:
    logging.info('Python HTTP trigger function processed a request.')

    try:
        # Load the model
        model = joblib.load('housing_model.pkl')

        # Get data from the request
        req_body = req.get_json()
        data = np.array(req_body['data']).reshape(1, -1)

        # Make prediction
        prediction = model.predict(data)

        return HttpResponse(json.dumps({'prediction': prediction.tolist()}), status_code=200)
    except Exception as e:
        logging.error(f"Error occurred: {e}")
        return HttpResponse(str(e), status_code=500)
```

3. Deploy to Azure: We deploy the function to Azure using Azure CLI or the Azure portal. Ensure the model file (`housing_model.pkl`) is included in the function app's deployment package.

```bash
az functionapp create --resource-group myResourceGroup --consumption-plan-location eastus --runtime python --runtime-version 3.8 --functions-version 3 --name myFunctionApp --storage-account myStorageAccount
```

Integrating AI with Other Azure Services

Azure provides a suite of services that can enhance AI applications:

- **Azure Cognitive Services:** Pre-built AI models for vision, speech, language, and decision-making tasks.

- **Azure Machine Learning:** A platform for training, deploying, and managing ML models.

- **Azure Event Grid**: A service for building event-driven architectures, useful for triggering functions based on events.

The Future of AI

The future of AI is bright, with ongoing research pushing the boundaries of what machines can achieve. Innovations in deep learning, natural language processing, and reinforcement learning continue to expand AI's capabilities. Serverless architectures will play a crucial role in this evolution, providing the scalability and flexibility needed to deploy complex AI systems.

The allure of artificial intelligence lies in its transformative potential across industries. By leveraging serverless machine learning and AI capabilities, developers can build scalable, cost-effective applications that harness the power of AI. Azure Functions, with its seamless integration into the Azure ecosystem, provides an ideal platform for deploying these applications. As AI continues to evolve, the possibilities for innovation are limitless, promising a future where intelligent systems enhance every aspect of our lives.

The Traditional AI Struggle: The Server Monster

Artificial Intelligence (AI) and Machine Learning (ML) have long promised to revolutionize industries by enabling systems to learn from data, adapt to new information, and automate complex tasks. However, traditional approaches to AI and ML often come with significant challenges, particularly when it comes to managing the underlying infrastructure—the so-called "server monster."

The Server Monster: Challenges in Traditional AI

In a traditional AI setup, managing servers is a critical yet cumbersome aspect. These challenges can be categorized into several key areas:

1. Scalability: Scaling AI workloads to handle large datasets or increased demand often requires substantial hardware investments and sophisticated load balancing strategies.

2. Cost: Maintaining physical or virtual servers for AI can be expensive, involving costs for hardware, electricity, cooling, and ongoing maintenance.

3. Complexity: Setting up and configuring servers, networking, storage, and security for AI applications requires specialized skills and significant time investment.

4. Maintenance: Regular updates, security patches, and performance tuning are necessary to keep servers running smoothly, diverting focus from core development activities.

5. Flexibility: Traditional server-based approaches can be inflexible, making it difficult to quickly adapt to changing workloads or integrate new technologies.

The Serverless Paradigm: A Solution to the Server Monster

Serverless computing, exemplified by services such as Azure Functions, offers a compelling solution to these challenges. In a serverless architecture, the cloud provider dynamically manages the allocation of machine resources, freeing developers from the need to manage servers.

Benefits of Serverless AI and ML

1. Scalability: Serverless platforms automatically scale to handle varying workloads, ensuring that applications remain responsive under different conditions without manual intervention.

2. Cost Efficiency: In a serverless model, you only pay for the actual compute time you use, eliminating the costs associated with idle servers.

3. Simplicity: Serverless abstracts away the complexity of infrastructure management, allowing developers to focus on writing code and developing models.

4. Maintenance-Free: The cloud provider handles maintenance tasks such as updates, security patches, and resource optimization.

5. Flexibility: Serverless architectures are highly flexible, enabling quick adaptation to changing workloads and easy integration of new services and technologies.

Implementing Serverless AI and ML with Azure Functions

Azure Functions is a serverless compute service from Microsoft Azure that allows developers to run code in response to events. Let's explore how to implement a serverless AI application using Azure Functions.

Example: Deploying a Machine Learning Model with Azure Functions

Suppose we have trained a machine learning model to predict customer churn based on various customer metrics. We can deploy this model using Azure Functions and make predictions via an HTTP endpoint.

1. Train the Model

First, we train a simple ML model using Python and scikit-learn.

```python
from sklearn.datasets import load_iris
from sklearn.model_selection import train_test_split
from sklearn.ensemble import RandomForestClassifier
import joblib

# Load dataset
iris = load_iris()
X = iris.data
y = iris.target

# Split data
X_train, X_test, y_train, y_test = train_test_split(X, y, test_size=0.2, random_state=42)
```

```
# Train model
model = RandomForestClassifier()
model.fit(X_train, y_train)

# Save model
joblib.dump(model, 'iris_model.pkl')
```

2. Create Azure Function

Next, we create an Azure Function to load the model and make predictions.

```python
import logging
import joblib
import json
import numpy as np
from azure.functions import HttpRequest, HttpResponse

# Load the model when the function starts
model = joblib.load('iris_model.pkl')

def main(req: HttpRequest) -> HttpResponse:
    logging.info('Python HTTP trigger function processed a request.')

    try:
```

```
# Get data from the request
req_body = req.get_json()
data = np.array(req_body['data']).reshape(1, -1)

# Make prediction
prediction = model.predict(data)

return HttpResponse(json.dumps({'prediction': prediction.tolist()}), status_code=200)
    except Exception as e:
        logging.error(f"Error occurred: {e}")
        return HttpResponse(str(e), status_code=500)
```

3. Deploy to Azure

Deploy the function to Azure using Azure CLI or the Azure portal. Ensure the model file (`iris_model.pkl`) is included in the function app's deployment package.

```bash
az functionapp create --resource-group myResourceGroup --consumption-plan-location eastus --runtime python --runtime-version 3.8 --functions-version 3 --name myFunctionApp --storage-account myStorageAccount
```

```
az functionapp deployment source config-zip --name
myFunctionApp --resource-group myResourceGroup --
src myfunction.zip
```

Integrating AI with Other Azure Services

Azure provides a comprehensive suite of services that can enhance AI applications, making them more powerful and easier to manage.

- **Azure Cognitive Services:** Pre-built AI models for vision, speech, language, and decision-making tasks, allowing developers to add sophisticated AI capabilities without building models from scratch.

- **Azure Machine Learning:** A platform for training, deploying, and managing ML models, which integrates seamlessly with Azure Functions for deploying serverless ML solutions.

- **Azure Event Grid:** A service for building event-driven architectures, which can trigger functions based on various events, enhancing the flexibility and responsiveness of AI applications.

Case Study: Real-World Application

Consider a retail company that wants to predict customer churn to implement retention strategies. Traditionally, this would require setting up and maintaining a complex server infrastructure to handle model training and prediction workloads. With serverless AI using Azure Functions, the company can deploy the churn prediction model as a serverless function, triggered by events such as customer data updates.

- **Event-Driven Triggers:** Azure Functions can be triggered by Azure Event Grid when new customer data is added or updated.

- **Real-Time Predictions:** The serverless function can process the data and return churn predictions in real-time, enabling the company to take immediate action.

- **Scalability and Cost-Efficiency:** The serverless architecture ensures the system scales automatically with demand and charges only for the compute time used, making it both scalable and cost-effective.

The Future of Serverless AI

The future of AI is closely tied to advancements in serverless computing. As AI models become more sophisticated and the demand for real-time processing grows, serverless architectures will play a crucial role in enabling scalable, cost-efficient, and flexible AI solutions. Innovations such as edge computing will further extend the capabilities of serverless AI, allowing for low-latency processing at the edge of the network.

The traditional AI struggle with the "server monster" presents significant challenges that can hinder innovation and efficiency. However, serverless computing, particularly with platforms like Azure Functions, offers a powerful solution. By abstracting away the complexities of infrastructure management, serverless architectures enable developers to focus on creating and deploying AI models that scale effortlessly and cost-effectively. The integration of AI and ML with serverless computing marks a significant advancement in the field, promising a future where intelligent, scalable applications can be deployed with unprecedented ease and efficiency.

Enter the Serverless Savior: Unleashing AI with Ease

Artificial Intelligence (AI) has long been hailed as the key to unlocking innovation and efficiency across industries. However, the path to harnessing the power of AI has been fraught with challenges, particularly when it comes to managing the underlying infrastructure. Enter serverless computing—a revolutionary paradigm that promises to simplify AI development, deployment, and scaling. In this article, we'll explore how serverless machine learning and AI are transforming the landscape of AI development, and how platforms like Azure Functions are leading the charge.

The Traditional AI Dilemma

Traditional AI development has often been hindered by the complexities of managing servers. From provisioning and scaling to maintenance and cost management, the "server monster" has loomed large, posing significant obstacles to innovation. Developers and data scientists have found themselves bogged down by infrastructure concerns, diverting valuable time and resources away from core AI development tasks.

The Promise of Serverless Machine Learning and AI

Serverless computing offers a compelling solution to the traditional AI dilemma. By abstracting away the complexities of infrastructure management, serverless platforms like Azure Functions empower developers to focus on what they do best—building and deploying AI models. With serverless machine learning and AI, developers can:

- **Scale Effortlessly:** Serverless platforms automatically scale to handle varying workloads, ensuring that AI applications remain responsive under different conditions without manual intervention.

- **Reduce Costs:** With serverless computing, developers only pay for the actual compute time used, eliminating the costs associated with idle servers and over-provisioning.

- **Simplify Development:** Serverless architectures abstract away the complexities of infrastructure management, allowing developers to focus on writing code and developing models.

- **Automate Maintenance:** The cloud provider handles maintenance tasks such as updates, security patches, and resource optimization, freeing developers from routine maintenance chores.

- **Enhance Flexibility:** Serverless architectures are highly flexible, enabling quick adaptation to changing workloads and easy integration of new services and technologies.

Implementing Serverless AI with Azure Functions

Azure Functions, a serverless compute service from Microsoft Azure, provides an ideal platform for deploying serverless AI applications. Let's explore how to implement a serverless AI application using Azure Functions.

Example: Deploying a Machine Learning Model with Azure Functions

Suppose we have trained a machine learning model to classify images of cats and dogs. We can deploy this model using Azure Functions and make predictions via an HTTP endpoint.

1. Train the Model

First, we train a simple machine learning model using Python and TensorFlow.

```python
import tensorflow as tf
from tensorflow.keras.preprocessing.image import ImageDataGenerator

# Load and preprocess data
train_datagen = ImageDataGenerator(rescale=1./255)
```

```python
train_generator = train_datagen.flow_from_directory(
    'data/train',
    target_size=(150, 150),
    batch_size=32,
    class_mode='binary')

# Define and train the model
model = tf.keras.models.Sequential([
    tf.keras.layers.Conv2D(32, (3, 3), activation='relu', input_shape=(150, 150, 3)),
    tf.keras.layers.MaxPooling2D(2, 2),
    tf.keras.layers.Conv2D(64, (3, 3), activation='relu'),
    tf.keras.layers.MaxPooling2D(2, 2),
    tf.keras.layers.Conv2D(128, (3, 3), activation='relu'),
    tf.keras.layers.MaxPooling2D(2, 2),
    tf.keras.layers.Conv2D(128, (3, 3), activation='relu'),
    tf.keras.layers.MaxPooling2D(2, 2),
    tf.keras.layers.Flatten(),
    tf.keras.layers.Dense(512, activation='relu'),
    tf.keras.layers.Dense(1, activation='sigmoid')
])

model.compile(loss='binary_crossentropy',
        optimizer=tf.keras.optimizers.RMSprop(lr=1e-4),
        metrics=['accuracy'])
```

```
model.fit(train_generator, steps_per_epoch=100, epochs=20)
```

2. Create Azure Function

Next, we create an Azure Function to load the trained model and make predictions.

```python
import logging
import tensorflow as tf
import numpy as np
from azure.functions import HttpRequest, HttpResponse

# Load the trained model
model = tf.keras.models.load_model('model.h5')

def main(req: HttpRequest) -> HttpResponse:
    logging.info('Python HTTP trigger function processed a request.')

    try:
        # Get image data from the request
        req_body = req.get_body()
        image = tf.image.decode_image(req_body)
        image = tf.image.resize(image, (150, 150))
        image = np.expand_dims(image, axis=0)
```

```
    # Make prediction
    prediction = model.predict(image)

    return HttpResponse(str(prediction[0][0]), status_code=200)
  except Exception as e:
    logging.error(f"Error occurred: {e}")
    return HttpResponse(str(e), status_code=500)
```

3. Deploy to Azure

Deploy the function to Azure using Azure CLI or the Azure portal.

```bash
az functionapp create --resource-group myResourceGroup --consumption-plan-location eastus --runtime python --runtime-version 3.8 --functions-version 3 --name myFunctionApp --storage-account myStorageAccount
```

Integrating Serverless AI with Other Azure Services

Azure provides a comprehensive suite of services that can enhance serverless AI applications, making them more powerful and easier to manage.

- **Azure Cognitive Services:** Pre-built AI models for vision, speech, language, and decision-making tasks, allowing developers to add sophisticated AI capabilities without building models from scratch.

- **Azure Machine Learning:** A platform for training, deploying, and managing ML models, which integrates seamlessly with Azure Functions for deploying serverless ML solutions.

- **Azure Event Grid:** A service for building event-driven architectures, which can trigger functions based on various events, enhancing the flexibility and responsiveness of serverless AI applications.

Case Study: Real-World Application

Consider a retail company that wants to automatically classify product images to improve search and recommendation features on their e-commerce platform. Traditionally, this would require setting up and maintaining a complex server infrastructure to handle image classification workloads. With serverless AI using Azure Functions, the company can deploy the image classification model as a serverless function, triggered by events such as new product uploads.

- **Event-Driven Triggers:** Azure Functions can be triggered by Azure Event Grid when new product images are uploaded.

- **Real-Time Predictions:** The serverless function can process the images and return classification results in real-time, enabling the company to enhance search and recommendation features.

- **Scalability and Cost-Efficiency:** The serverless architecture ensures the system scales automatically with demand and charges only for the compute time used, making it both scalable and cost-effective.

The Future of Serverless AI

The future of AI is closely tied to advancements in serverless computing. As AI models become more sophisticated and the demand for real-time processing grows, serverless architectures will play a crucial role in enabling scalable, cost-efficient, and flexible AI solutions. Innovations such as edge computing will further extend the capabilities of serverless AI, allowing for low-latency processing at the edge of the network.

Serverless machine learning and AI offer a transformative approach to AI development, simplifying infrastructure management and empowering developers to focus on building and deploying sophisticated AI applications with ease. With platforms like Azure Functions leading the charge, developers can leverage serverless computing to scale their AI solutions effortlessly, reduce costs, and simplify development and maintenance. The integration of serverless AI with other Azure services further enhances the capabilities of AI applications, making them more powerful and responsive to changing business needs.

As we look to the future, the possibilities for serverless AI are boundless. From enhancing customer experiences in retail and e-commerce to improving healthcare outcomes and driving innovation in manufacturing and logistics, serverless AI has the potential to revolutionize industries across the globe. By embracing serverless computing and AI, organizations can unlock new opportunities for growth, efficiency, and innovation, positioning themselves for success in the digital age.

The emergence of serverless computing as a savior for AI development represents a significant milestone in the evolution of artificial intelligence. With serverless machine learning and AI, developers can unleash the full potential of AI without being bogged down by the complexities of infrastructure management. As serverless AI continues to mature and evolve, we can expect to see even greater advancements in AI-driven applications, paving the way for a future where intelligent, scalable, and cost-effective AI solutions are within reach for organizations of all sizes.

Chapter 2

The Power of Serverless Computing for AI

What is Serverless Computing?

Serverless computing is a cloud computing model that abstracts away the management of servers, allowing developers to focus solely on writing and deploying code without worrying about provisioning, scaling, or managing infrastructure. In a serverless architecture, cloud providers dynamically allocate resources to execute code in response to events or triggers, such as HTTP requests, database changes, or timer-based schedules. This paradigm shift in computing offers several benefits, including scalability, cost-efficiency, and simplified development, making it an attractive option for building modern applications, including those leveraging machine learning and artificial intelligence.

Key Characteristics of Serverless Computing:

1. Event-Driven Execution: Serverless functions are triggered by events or triggers, such as HTTP requests, database changes, file uploads, or timer-based schedules. Each function is executed in response to a specific event, enabling event-driven architectures.

2. No Server Management: With serverless computing, developers are relieved of the burden of managing servers, operating systems, or runtime environments. Cloud providers handle infrastructure provisioning, scaling, and maintenance, allowing developers to focus on writing code.

3. Auto-Scaling: Serverless platforms automatically scale resources up or down based on workload demands. Functions are instantiated and scaled dynamically in response to incoming requests, ensuring optimal performance and resource utilization.

4. Pay-Per-Use Pricing: Serverless computing follows a pay-per-use pricing model, where developers are charged only for the compute time and resources consumed by their functions. This model eliminates the need for upfront hardware investments and allows for cost-efficient scaling.

5. Stateless Execution: Serverless functions are typically stateless, meaning they do not maintain state between invocations. Any required state must be managed externally, such as in a database or external storage service.

Serverless Machine Learning and Artificial Intelligence:

Serverless computing has opened up new possibilities for deploying machine learning and artificial intelligence applications. By leveraging serverless platforms, developers can deploy machine learning models and AI algorithms as serverless functions, enabling real-time predictions, data processing, and intelligent automation without the need for managing infrastructure. Let's explore how serverless computing is transforming the landscape of machine learning and artificial intelligence:

Scalability:

Serverless platforms, such as Azure Functions, automatically scale resources to handle varying workloads, making them well-suited for machine learning tasks that require processing large datasets or serving predictions to a high volume of users. With serverless machine learning, developers can deploy models that scale effortlessly to meet demand, ensuring consistent performance and responsiveness.

Cost-Efficiency:

Serverless computing follows a pay-per-use pricing model, where developers are billed only for the compute time and resources consumed by their functions. This makes serverless machine learning cost-effective, particularly for sporadic or unpredictable workloads. Developers can avoid the overhead of provisioning and managing dedicated infrastructure, reducing operational costs and maximizing resource utilization.

Simplified Development:

Serverless platforms abstract away the complexities of infrastructure management, allowing developers to focus on writing code and developing models. With serverless machine learning, developers can streamline the deployment process, deploying models with a few simple commands or clicks in the cloud console. This accelerates time-to-market and enables rapid experimentation and iteration in AI development.

Implementing Serverless Machine Learning with Azure Functions:

Azure Functions, a serverless computer service provided by Microsoft Azure, offers a powerful platform for deploying serverless machine learning applications. Let's explore how to implement serverless machine learning with Azure Functions using a simple example:

Example: Deploying a Machine Learning Model with Azure Functions

Suppose we have trained a machine learning model to classify images of flowers. We can deploy this model as a serverless function using Azure Functions and make predictions via an HTTP endpoint.

1. Train the Model: First, we train a simple machine learning model using Python and TensorFlow.

```python
import tensorflow as tf
from tensorflow.keras.preprocessing.image import ImageDataGenerator

# Load and preprocess data
train_datagen = ImageDataGenerator(rescale=1./255)
train_generator = train_datagen.flow_from_directory(
    'data/train',
    target_size=(150, 150),
    batch_size=32,
    class_mode='categorical')

# Define and train the model
model = tf.keras.models.Sequential([
    tf.keras.layers.Conv2D(32, (3, 3), activation='relu', input_shape=(150, 150, 3)),
    tf.keras.layers.MaxPooling2D(2, 2),
    tf.keras.layers.Conv2D(64, (3, 3), activation='relu'),
    tf.keras.layers.MaxPooling2D(2, 2),
```

```
    tf.keras.layers.Conv2D(128, (3, 3), activation='relu'),
    tf.keras.layers.MaxPooling2D(2, 2),
    tf.keras.layers.Conv2D(128, (3, 3), activation='relu'),
    tf.keras.layers.MaxPooling2D(2, 2),
    tf.keras.layers.Flatten(),
    tf.keras.layers.Dense(512, activation='relu'),
    tf.keras.layers.Dense(5, activation='softmax')
])

model.compile(loss='categorical_crossentropy', optimizer=tf.keras.optimizers.RMSprop(lr=1e-4), metrics=['accuracy'])

model.fit(train_generator, steps_per_epoch=100, epochs=20)
```

2. Create Azure Function: Next, we create an Azure Function to load the trained model and make predictions.

```python
import logging
import tensorflow as tf
import numpy as np
```

```python
from azure.functions import HttpRequest, HttpResponse

# Load the trained model
model = tf.keras.models.load_model('flower_model.h5')

def main(req: HttpRequest) -> HttpResponse:
    logging.info('Python HTTP trigger function processed a request.')

    try:
        # Get image data from the request
        req_body = req.get_body()
        image = tf.image.decode_image(req_body)
        image = tf.image.resize(image, (150, 150))
        image = np.expand_dims(image, axis=0)

        # Make prediction
        prediction = model.predict(image)

        return HttpResponse(str(prediction), status_code=200)
    except Exception as e:
        logging.error(f"Error occurred: {e}")
        return HttpResponse(str(e), status_code=500)
```

3. Deploy to Azure: Deploy the function to Azure using Azure CLI or the Azure portal.

```bash
az functionapp create --resource-group myResourceGroup --consumption-plan-location eastus --runtime python --runtime-version 3.8 --functions-version 3 --name myFunctionApp --storage-account myStorageAccount
```

Serverless computing represents a paradigm shift in the way developers build and deploy applications, offering scalability, cost-efficiency, and simplified development. With serverless machine learning and artificial intelligence, developers can leverage the power of AI without the complexity of managing infrastructure. Platforms like Azure Functions provide a flexible and scalable environment for deploying serverless AI applications, enabling organizations to unlock new opportunities for innovation and growth. As serverless computing continues to evolve, we can expect to see even greater advancements in AI-driven applications, transforming industries and driving the next wave of technological innovation.

The Pay-as-You-Go Advantage: Serverless Machine Learning and Artificial Intelligence

In the realm of technology, efficiency and cost-effectiveness are paramount. Enter serverless computing—a revolutionary approach that not only simplifies development but also offers a pay-as-you-go advantage. With the rise of serverless machine learning and artificial intelligence (AI), developers can leverage this paradigm to build scalable, cost-efficient AI applications without the burden of managing infrastructure. In this article, we'll explore the pay-as-you-go advantage of serverless computing, delve into serverless machine learning and AI, and showcase how platforms like Azure Functions enable developers to harness this transformative technology.

Understanding the Pay-as-You-Go Model:

The pay-as-you-go model, also known as consumption-based pricing, allows users to pay only for the resources and services they consume, rather than committing to a fixed monthly fee or upfront costs. This model aligns costs with usage, providing flexibility and cost-efficiency, particularly for fluctuating workloads. In the context of serverless computing, the pay-as-you-go advantage extends to serverless machine learning and AI, offering several key benefits:

1. Cost-Efficiency: With pay-as-you-go pricing, users are charged only for the compute time and resources consumed by their applications. This eliminates the need for upfront hardware investments or over-provisioning, resulting in significant cost savings, especially for sporadic or unpredictable workloads.

2. Scalability: Serverless platforms automatically scale resources up or down based on workload demands, ensuring optimal performance and resource utilization. Users can seamlessly handle fluctuations in traffic or workload without manual intervention, enabling scalability without the associated costs of maintaining idle resources.

3. Flexibility: The pay-as-you-go model offers flexibility in resource allocation, allowing users to adjust resources based on changing requirements or business needs. Users can scale resources dynamically in response to spikes in demand or scale down during periods of low activity, optimizing costs without sacrificing performance.

Implementing Serverless Machine Learning and AI:

Serverless computing has democratized access to AI and machine learning, making it easier for developers to deploy and scale intelligent applications. Let's explore how to leverage the pay-as-you-go advantage of serverless computing for machine learning and AI:

Scalability and Cost-Efficiency:

Serverless machine learning and AI applications can benefit significantly from the scalability and cost-efficiency of the pay-as-you-go model. By deploying AI models as serverless functions, developers can automatically scale resources to handle varying workloads, ensuring consistent performance and responsiveness. With pay-as-you-go pricing, developers only pay for the compute time and resources consumed by their functions, eliminating the costs associated with idle servers or over-provisioned infrastructure.

Simplified Development:

The pay-as-you-go model simplifies the development and deployment of serverless machine learning and AI applications. With platforms like Azure Functions, developers can focus on writing code and developing models without worrying about provisioning or managing infrastructure. By abstracting away the complexities of infrastructure management, serverless computing enables rapid development and iteration, accelerating time-to-market and fostering innovation in AI development.

Example: Deploying a Serverless AI Application with Azure Functions:

Let's consider an example of deploying a sentiment analysis model as a serverless function using Azure Functions:

1. Train the Model: First, we train a sentiment analysis model using Python and natural language processing techniques.

```python
import nltk
from nltk.sentiment.vader import SentimentIntensityAnalyzer

# Train the sentiment analysis model
nltk.download('vader_lexicon')
analyzer = SentimentIntensityAnalyzer()
```

2. Create Azure Function: Next, we create an Azure Function to analyze sentiment using the trained model.

```python
```

```python
import logging
from azure.functions import HttpRequest, HttpResponse

def main(req: HttpRequest) -> HttpResponse:
    logging.info('Python HTTP trigger function processed a request.')

    try:
        # Get text data from the request
        req_body = req.get_json()
        text = req_body['text']

        # Analyze sentiment
        sentiment = analyzer.polarity_scores(text)

        return HttpResponse(str(sentiment), status_code=200)
    except Exception as e:
        logging.error(f"Error occurred: {e}")
        return HttpResponse(str(e), status_code=500)
```

3. **Deploy to Azure:** Deploy the function to Azure using Azure CLI or the Azure portal.

```bash
```

```
az functionapp create --resource-group myResourceGroup --consumption-plan-location eastus --runtime python --runtime-version 3.8 --functions-version 3 --name myFunctionApp --storage-account myStorageAccount
```

The pay-as-you-go advantage of serverless computing revolutionizes the way developers build and deploy AI and machine learning applications. By leveraging scalable, cost-efficient serverless platforms like Azure Functions, developers can unlock new opportunities for innovation and growth. With the pay-as-you-go model, developers only pay for the compute time and resources consumed by their applications, making serverless computing an attractive option for organizations seeking to optimize costs and maximize efficiency. As serverless machine learning and AI continue to evolve, the pay-as-you-go advantage will play a crucial role in driving the next wave of technological innovation, empowering developers to build intelligent applications that scale seamlessly and cost-effect

Scaling Without the Stress: Serverless Machine Learning and Artificial Intelligence

In the fast-paced world of technology, the ability to scale applications seamlessly is essential for success. With the emergence of serverless computing, scaling applications—especially those leveraging machine learning (ML) and artificial intelligence (AI)—has become significantly easier and more efficient. In this article, we'll explore how serverless computing enables scaling without the stress, delve into serverless ML and AI, and demonstrate how platforms like Azure Functions empower developers to build scalable intelligent applications with ease.

Understanding Scaling in Serverless Computing:

Scaling in serverless computing refers to the ability to handle increased workloads or traffic by automatically provisioning resources in response to demand. Unlike traditional architectures, where scaling often involves manual intervention or pre-provisioning of resources, serverless platforms dynamically allocate resources based on workload requirements, allowing applications to scale seamlessly without the need for human intervention. This "auto-scaling" capability is one of the key advantages of serverless computing and is particularly beneficial for applications with unpredictable or fluctuating workloads, such as those in ML and AI.

The Stress-Free Scaling Advantage:

Scaling without the stress is a significant advantage of serverless computing, offering several key benefits:

1. Automatic Scaling: Serverless platforms, such as Azure Functions, automatically scale resources up or down based on workload demands. This means that applications can handle spikes in traffic or workload without manual intervention, ensuring optimal performance and availability under varying conditions.

2. Cost-Efficiency: With automatic scaling, developers only pay for the compute time and resources consumed by their applications. This eliminates the need for over-provisioning or maintaining idle resources, resulting in cost savings and improved resource utilization.

3. Simplified Management: Serverless platforms abstract away the complexities of infrastructure management, allowing developers to focus on writing code and building applications. Scaling is handled transparently by the platform, reducing the operational burden on developers and eliminating the need for manual intervention.

Scaling Serverless Machine Learning and AI:

Scaling ML and AI applications can be challenging due to the computational resources required for training and inference tasks. Serverless computing offers a scalable and cost-effective solution for deploying ML and AI models, enabling developers to scale applications seamlessly without worrying about infrastructure constraints. Let's explore how to scale serverless ML and AI applications using Azure Functions:

Scalable Model Training:

With serverless ML, developers can leverage platforms like Azure Functions to distribute training workloads across multiple function instances, allowing for parallel processing and faster model training. By breaking down training tasks into smaller, independent units, developers can scale model training horizontally, ensuring efficient resource utilization and reduced training times.

Elastic Inference:

Serverless platforms offer elastic inference capabilities, allowing developers to dynamically allocate resources for model inference based on demand. With Azure Functions, developers can configure functions to scale up or down based on the number of incoming requests, ensuring optimal performance and responsiveness for inference tasks.

Real-Time Prediction Scaling:

For applications requiring real-time predictions, serverless platforms offer the ability to scale prediction endpoints dynamically based on incoming traffic. With Azure Functions, developers can deploy prediction endpoints as serverless functions and configure them to scale automatically in response to changes in workload, ensuring consistent performance and availability for end users.

Implementing Scaling with Azure Functions:

Let's consider an example of scaling a sentiment analysis application using Azure Functions:

1. Train the Model: First, we train a sentiment analysis model using Python and TensorFlow.

```python
import tensorflow as tf
import numpy as np

# Load and preprocess data
# Code for data loading and preprocessing goes here

# Define and train the model
model = tf.keras.models.Sequential([
    # Model architecture goes here
```

```python
])

model.compile(loss='binary_crossentropy',
          optimizer='adam',
          metrics=['accuracy'])

model.fit(X_train, y_train, epochs=10, batch_size=32)
```

2. Create Azure Function: Next, we create an Azure Function to perform sentiment analysis using the trained model.

```python
import logging
import tensorflow as tf
from azure.functions import HttpRequest, HttpResponse

# Load the trained model
model = tf.keras.models.load_model('sentiment_model.h5')

def main(req: HttpRequest) -> HttpResponse:
    logging.info('Python HTTP trigger function processed a request.')

    try:
```

```python
    # Get text data from the request
    req_body = req.get_json()
    text = req_body['text']

    # Perform sentiment analysis
    prediction = model.predict([text])

    return HttpResponse(str(prediction), status_code=200)
  except Exception as e:
    logging.error(f"Error occurred: {e}")
    return HttpResponse(str(e), status_code=500)
```

3. Deploy to Azure: Deploy the function to Azure using Azure CLI or the Azure portal.

```bash
az functionapp create --resource-group myResourceGroup --consumption-plan-location eastus --runtime python --runtime-version 3.8 --functions-version 3 --name myFunctionApp --storage-account myStorageAccount
```

Scaling without the stress is a game-changer for ML and AI applications, and serverless computing makes it possible. With automatic scaling, cost-efficiency, and simplified management, serverless platforms like Azure Functions enable developers to build scalable intelligent applications with ease. By leveraging the scaling capabilities of serverless computing, developers can focus on building innovative ML and AI solutions without worrying about infrastructure constraints, empowering them to unlock new possibilities and drive digital transformation in various industries. As serverless ML and AI continue to evolve, the stress-free scaling advantage will play a crucial role in accelerating the adoption and success of intelligent applications across the globe.

Serverless vs. Traditional AI Development: A Game Changer

In the ever-evolving landscape of technology, the advent of serverless computing has revolutionized the way developers approach application development. This paradigm shift extends to the field of artificial intelligence (AI) and machine learning (ML), offering a game-changing alternative to traditional development methods. In this article, we'll compare serverless AI development with traditional approaches, explore the benefits and challenges of each, and showcase how serverless machine learning and AI are transforming the industry.

Understanding Traditional AI Development:

Traditional AI development typically involves setting up and managing infrastructure to train, deploy, and maintain machine learning models. This approach requires developers to provision servers, install software dependencies, manage scalability and resource allocation, and handle infrastructure maintenance tasks. While traditional AI development provides granular control over the underlying infrastructure, it often comes with inherent complexities and challenges, including:

- **Infrastructure Management:** Developers are responsible for provisioning and managing servers, databases, and other infrastructure components required for AI development.

- **Scalability**: Scaling traditional AI applications to handle increased workloads or traffic can be challenging and may require manual intervention or pre-provisioning of resources.

- **Cost**: Traditional AI development incurs upfront costs for hardware, software licenses, and infrastructure maintenance, making it less flexible and cost-efficient, especially for small-scale projects or experimental use cases.

Introducing Serverless AI Development:

Serverless AI development, on the other hand, leverages serverless computing platforms to abstract away the complexities of infrastructure management, allowing developers to focus on writing code and building intelligent applications. With serverless machine learning and AI, developers can deploy, scale, and manage AI models without worrying about provisioning servers or managing infrastructure. This approach offers several key benefits:

- **Simplified Development:** Serverless platforms, such as Azure Functions, abstract away the complexities of infrastructure management, allowing developers to focus on writing code and building AI applications.

- **Auto-Scaling:** Serverless platforms automatically scale resources up or down based on workload demands, ensuring optimal performance and resource utilization without manual intervention.

- **Cost-Efficiency:** Serverless computing follows a pay-as-you-go pricing model, where developers only pay for the compute time and resources consumed by their applications, eliminating the need for upfront hardware investments or over-provisioning.

Comparing Serverless vs. Traditional AI Development:

Let's compare serverless AI development with traditional approaches across various aspects:

1. Infrastructure Management:

- **Traditional AI Development:** Requires developers to provision and manage servers, databases, and other infrastructure components.

- **Serverless AI Development:** Abstracts away infrastructure management, allowing developers to focus on writing code and building applications.

2. Scalability:

- **Traditional AI Development:** Scaling traditional AI applications can be challenging and may require manual intervention or pre-provisioning of resources.

- **Serverless AI Development:** Serverless platforms automatically scale resources based on workload demands, ensuring optimal performance and resource utilization without manual intervention.

3. **Cost:**

    - **Traditional AI Development:** Incurs upfront costs for hardware, software licenses, and infrastructure maintenance.

    - **Serverless AI Development:** Follows a pay-as-you-go pricing model, where developers only pay for the compute time and resources consumed by their applications, resulting in cost savings and improved resource utilization.

Implementing Serverless AI with Azure Functions:

Let's consider an example of implementing a sentiment analysis application using Azure Functions for serverless AI development:

1. Train the Model: Train a sentiment analysis model using Python and TensorFlow.

2. Create Azure Function: Create an Azure Function to perform sentiment analysis using the trained model.

3. Deploy to Azure: Deploy the function to Azure using Azure CLI or the Azure portal.

```python
import logging
import tensorflow as tf
from azure.functions import HttpRequest, HttpResponse

# Load the trained model
model = tf.keras.models.load_model('sentiment_model.h5')

def main(req: HttpRequest) -> HttpResponse:
    logging.info('Python HTTP trigger function processed a request.')

    try:
        # Get text data from the request
        req_body = req.get_json()
        text = req_body['text']

        # Perform sentiment analysis
        prediction = model.predict([text])
```

```
        return HttpResponse(str(prediction), status_code=200)
    except Exception as e:
        logging.error(f"Error occurred: {e}")
        return HttpResponse(str(e), status_code=500)
```

Serverless AI development represents a game-changing approach to building intelligent applications, offering simplified development, auto-scaling, and cost-efficiency compared to traditional methods. By abstracting away infrastructure management and automating scalability, serverless platforms like Azure Functions empower developers to focus on innovation and accelerate the adoption of AI and machine learning across various industries. As serverless AI continues to evolve, it will play a crucial role in driving the next wave of technological innovation and transforming the way we build and deploy intelligent applications.

Who Benefits from Serverless AI? (Spoiler Alert: Everyone!)

Serverless computing has democratized access to artificial intelligence (AI) and machine learning (ML), making it easier for organizations and individuals to leverage intelligent applications without the burden of managing infrastructure. In this article, we'll explore how serverless AI benefits various stakeholders, including developers, businesses, end-users, and society as a whole. We'll delve into real-world examples and showcase how serverless machine learning and AI are transforming industries and driving innovation across the globe.

Developers: Empowering Innovation

Serverless AI empowers developers to innovate and build intelligent applications without the complexities of infrastructure management. By abstracting away infrastructure concerns, serverless platforms like Azure Functions enable developers to focus on writing code, experimenting with AI models, and delivering value to end-users. With serverless computing, developers can accelerate the development cycle, iterate rapidly, and bring AI-powered solutions to market faster than ever before.

Example: Sentiment Analysis Application

Consider a developer building a sentiment analysis application using Azure Functions. By leveraging serverless machine learning, the developer can deploy a sentiment analysis model as a serverless function, enabling real-time analysis of text data without worrying about provisioning servers or managing infrastructure. This empowers the developer to focus on refining the model, improving accuracy, and enhancing the user experience, rather than getting bogged down by infrastructure concerns.

```python
import logging
import tensorflow as tf
from azure.functions import HttpRequest, HttpResponse

# Load the trained model
model = tf.keras.models.load_model('sentiment_model.h5')

def main(req: HttpRequest) -> HttpResponse:
    logging.info('Python HTTP trigger function processed a request.')

    try:
        # Get text data from the request
        req_body = req.get_json()
        text = req_body['text']

        # Perform sentiment analysis
        prediction = model.predict([text])

        return HttpResponse(str(prediction), status_code=200)
    except Exception as e:
```

```
logging.error(f"Error occurred: {e}")
return HttpResponse(str(e), status_code=500)
```
```

## Businesses: Driving Innovation and Growth

Businesses across industries are leveraging serverless AI to drive innovation, improve efficiency, and gain a competitive edge in the market. From startups to large enterprises, organizations can harness the power of serverless machine learning and AI to streamline processes, automate tasks, and deliver personalized experiences to customers. By adopting serverless AI, businesses can unlock new opportunities for growth, optimize operations, and transform the way they operate in the digital age.

## Example: E-commerce Recommendation Engine

An e-commerce company can use serverless AI to deploy a recommendation engine that provides personalized product recommendations to customers. By analyzing past purchase history, browsing behavior, and demographic data, the recommendation engine can generate tailored product suggestions in real-time, increasing customer engagement and driving sales. With serverless computing, the company can scale the recommendation engine dynamically to handle varying
```

traffic loads during peak shopping seasons, ensuring optimal performance and responsiveness for shoppers.

End-Users: Enhancing Experiences

End-users are the ultimate beneficiaries of serverless AI, as they enjoy enhanced experiences, personalized services, and intelligent features powered by AI and machine learning. Whether it's intelligent chatbots, recommendation systems, or predictive analytics, end-users benefit from the seamless integration of AI into everyday applications, making their lives easier, more convenient, and more enjoyable.

Example: Virtual Assistant

A virtual assistant powered by serverless AI can provide personalized assistance to users, helping them with tasks such as scheduling appointments, setting reminders, and answering questions. By leveraging natural language processing and machine learning algorithms, the virtual assistant can understand user queries, provide relevant information, and adapt to user preferences over time. With serverless computing, the virtual assistant can scale dynamically to handle increased demand, ensuring a smooth and responsive user experience.

Society: Driving Positive Impact

Serverless AI has the potential to drive positive societal impact by addressing complex challenges, improving accessibility, and advancing social causes. From healthcare and education to environmental conservation and humanitarian efforts, serverless AI can be used to tackle pressing issues, empower marginalized communities, and drive positive change on a global scale.

Example: Healthcare Diagnostics

In healthcare, serverless AI can be used to develop diagnostic tools that assist healthcare professionals in detecting and diagnosing diseases. By analyzing medical imaging data, genetic information, and patient records, AI-powered diagnostic systems can identify patterns, detect abnormalities, and provide early detection of diseases such as cancer and cardiovascular conditions. With serverless computing, these diagnostic tools can be deployed cost-effectively, making them accessible to healthcare facilities in underserved areas and improving healthcare outcomes for patients worldwide.

Serverless AI benefits everyone—developers, businesses, end-users, and society as a whole—by empowering innovation, driving growth, enhancing experiences, and driving positive societal impact. By abstracting away infrastructure concerns and providing scalable, cost-effective computing resources, serverless platforms enable organizations and individuals to harness the power of AI and machine learning and unlock new opportunities for innovation and growth. As serverless AI continues to evolve, we can expect to see even greater advancements in technology, transforming industries, shaping the future, and driving positive change for generations to come.

Chapter 3

Top Cloud Platforms for Serverless AI Development

AWS Lambda: The Serverless Powerhouse for Machine Learning and AI

In the era of cloud computing, AWS Lambda emerged as a dominant force, providing developers with a powerful platform for building and deploying serverless applications. With its seamless integration with other AWS services, robust scalability, and pay-as-you-go pricing model, AWS Lambda is a go-to choice for implementing serverless machine learning (ML) and artificial intelligence (AI) applications. In this article, we'll explore the features and capabilities of AWS Lambda, delve into its use cases in serverless ML and AI, and showcase how developers can leverage its power with code examples.

Understanding AWS Lambda:

AWS Lambda is a serverless compute service offered by Amazon Web Services (AWS) that enables developers to run code without provisioning or managing servers. With Lambda, developers can upload their code as functions and define triggers to execute them in response to events such as HTTP requests, changes to data in Amazon S3,

DynamoDB, or SNS notifications. Lambda automatically scales resources to handle incoming requests, ensuring optimal performance and cost-efficiency.

Key Features of AWS Lambda:

1. Pay-as-You-Go Pricing: AWS Lambda follows a pay-as-you-go pricing model, where developers are charged only for the compute time and resources consumed by their functions, with no upfront costs or minimum fees.

2. Auto-Scaling: Lambda automatically scales resources up or down based on workload demands, ensuring that functions have access to the right amount of compute power to handle incoming requests.

3. Integration with AWS Services: Lambda seamlessly integrates with other AWS services, allowing developers to build event-driven architectures and automate workflows by connecting functions to services like Amazon S3, DynamoDB, SQS, and more.

4. Multi-Language Support: Lambda supports multiple programming languages, including Python, Node.js, Java, C#, and Go, giving developers the flexibility to choose the language that best suits their needs.

Serverless Machine Learning and AI with AWS Lambda:

AWS Lambda provides a robust platform for deploying serverless ML and AI applications, offering scalability, cost-efficiency, and seamless integration with other AWS services. Let's explore some common use cases of AWS Lambda in serverless ML and AI:

1. Model Inference: Lambda functions can be used to deploy ML models for inference, enabling real-time predictions without managing servers or infrastructure. By integrating Lambda with AWS SageMaker or TensorFlow Serving, developers can deploy trained models as serverless functions and invoke them via HTTP endpoints or event triggers.

2. Data Processing: Lambda functions can preprocess data before feeding it into ML models. For example, developers can use Lambda to resize images, extract features, or clean and normalize data before training or inference.

3. Chatbots and Natural Language Processing (NLP): Lambda functions can power chatbots and NLP applications, automating customer support, analyzing user feedback, or extracting insights from text data. By integrating Lambda with Amazon Lex or Amazon Comprehend, developers can build intelligent conversational interfaces that understand and respond to natural language queries.

Example: Image Classification with AWS Lambda and Amazon Rekognition

Let's consider an example of deploying an image classification application using AWS Lambda and Amazon Rekognition:

1. Upload Image to Amazon S3: Users upload images to an Amazon S3 bucket.

2. Trigger Lambda Function: An S3 event triggers a Lambda function, responsible for invoking the Amazon Rekognition API to analyze and classify the image.

3. Process Image: The Lambda function retrieves the image from S3, calls the Amazon Rekognition API to perform image classification, and returns the results.

4. Display Results: The results of the image classification are displayed to the user via a web interface or mobile application.

Code Example: Deploying a Lambda Function for Image Classification

Let's write a simple Lambda function using Python to perform image classification with the Amazon Rekognition API:

```python
import boto3

def lambda_handler(event, context):
    # Initialize the Amazon Rekognition client
    rekognition = boto3.client('rekognition')

    # Retrieve the S3 bucket and key from the event
    bucket = event['Records'][0]['s3']['bucket']['name']
    key = event['Records'][0]['s3']['object']['key']

    # Call the detect_labels API to perform image classification
    response = rekognition.detect_labels(
        Image={
            'S3Object': {
                'Bucket': bucket,
                'Name': key
            },
            MaxLabels=10
        )
```

```
    # Extract and return the labels
    labels = [label['Name'] for label in response['Labels']]
    return labels
```

AWS Lambda serves as a powerhouse for serverless machine learning and artificial intelligence, providing developers with a flexible and scalable platform to deploy intelligent applications. With its pay-as-you-go pricing model, auto-scaling capabilities, and seamless integration with other AWS services, Lambda enables developers to focus on building innovative solutions without worrying about managing infrastructure. By leveraging Lambda, developers can accelerate the pace of innovation and drive the adoption of ML and AI across industries. As Lambda continues to evolve, we can expect to see even greater advancements in serverless computing and AI, shaping the future of technology and unlocking new possibilities for developers and organizations alike.

Google Cloud Functions: A Flexible Option for Serverless ML and AI

In the realm of serverless computing, Google Cloud Functions stands out as a versatile and powerful option for deploying machine learning (ML) and artificial intelligence (AI) applications. With its seamless integration with other Google Cloud services, robust scalability, and support for multiple programming languages, Google Cloud Functions provides developers with a flexible platform to build and deploy intelligent applications without the hassle of managing infrastructure. In this article, we'll explore the features and capabilities of Google Cloud Functions, delve into its use cases in serverless ML and AI, and demonstrate how developers can leverage its flexibility with code examples.

Understanding Google Cloud Functions:

Google Cloud Functions is a serverless compute service offered by Google Cloud Platform (GCP) that enables developers to run code in response to events without provisioning or managing servers. With Cloud Functions, developers can upload their code as functions and define triggers to execute them in response to events such as HTTP requests, changes to data in Google Cloud Storage, Firestore, Pub/Sub messages, or HTTP requests. Cloud Functions automatically scales resources to handle incoming requests, ensuring optimal performance and cost-efficiency.

Key Features of Google Cloud Functions:

1. Pay-as-You-Go Pricing: Google Cloud Functions follows a pay-as-you-go pricing model, where developers are charged only for the compute time and resources consumed by their functions, with no upfront costs or minimum fees.

2. Auto-Scaling: Cloud Functions automatically scales resources up or down based on workload demands, ensuring that functions have access to the right amount of compute power to handle incoming requests.

3. Integration with Google Cloud Services: Cloud Functions seamlessly integrates with other Google Cloud services, allowing developers to build event-driven architectures and automate workflows by connecting functions to services like Cloud Storage, Firestore, Pub/Sub, BigQuery, and more.

4. Multi-Language Support: Cloud Functions supports multiple programming languages, including Node.js, Python, Go, Java, and .NET, giving developers the flexibility to choose the language that best suits their needs.

Serverless Machine Learning and AI with Google Cloud Functions:

Google Cloud Functions is an excellent choice for deploying serverless ML and AI applications, offering scalability, cost-efficiency, and seamless integration with other Google Cloud services. Let's explore some common use cases of Google Cloud Functions in serverless ML and AI:

1. Model Inference: Cloud Functions can be used to deploy ML models for inference, enabling real-time predictions without managing servers or infrastructure. By integrating Cloud Functions with Google Cloud AI Platform or TensorFlow Serving, developers can deploy trained models as serverless functions and invoke them via HTTP endpoints or event triggers.

2. Data Processing: Cloud Functions can preprocess data before feeding it into ML models. For example, developers can use Cloud Functions to resize images, extract features, or clean and normalize data before training or inference.

3. Chatbots and Natural Language Processing (NLP): Cloud Functions can power chatbots and NLP applications, automating customer support, analyzing user feedback, or extracting insights from text data. By integrating Cloud Functions with Dialog Flow or Cloud Natural Language API, developers can build intelligent conversational interfaces that understand and respond to natural language queries.

Example: Image Classification with Google Cloud Functions and Cloud Vision API

Let's consider an example of deploying an image classification application using Google Cloud Functions and Cloud Vision API:

1. Upload Image to Google Cloud Storage: Users upload images to a Google Cloud Storage bucket.

2. Trigger Cloud Function: An event in Cloud Storage triggers a Cloud Function, responsible for invoking the Cloud Vision API to analyze and classify the image.

3. Process Image: The Cloud Function retrieves the image from Cloud Storage, calls the Cloud Vision API to perform image classification, and returns the results.

4. Display Results: The results of the image classification are displayed to the user via a web interface or mobile application.

Code Example: Deploying a Cloud Function for Image Classification

Let's write a simple Cloud Function using Python to perform image classification with the Cloud Vision API:

```python
import base64
from google.cloud import vision

def classify_image(data, context):
    client = vision.ImageAnnotatorClient()

    # Get image data from the Cloud Storage event
    file_data = data['data']
    image_bytes = base64.b64decode(file_data)

    # Perform image classification
    image = vision.Image(content=image_bytes)
    response = client.label_detection(image=image)
    labels = response.label_annotations

    # Print labels
    for label in labels:
        print(label.description)
```

Google Cloud Functions offers developers a flexible and powerful platform for deploying serverless ML and AI applications. With its pay-as-you-go pricing model, auto-scaling capabilities, and seamless integration with other

Google Cloud services, Cloud Functions enables developers to focus on building intelligent applications without worrying about managing infrastructure. By leveraging Cloud Functions, developers can accelerate the pace of innovation and drive the adoption of AI and ML across industries. As Cloud Functions continues to evolve, we can expect to see even greater advancements in serverless computing and AI, empowering developers to unlock new possibilities and drive digital transformation on a global scale. With its ease of use, robust features, and extensive ecosystem of services, Google Cloud Functions is indeed a flexible option for developers looking to harness the power of serverless machine learning and artificial intelligence. Whether it's deploying ML models for inference, processing data, or building intelligent chatbots, Cloud Functions provides a scalable and cost-effective platform to bring innovative AI solutions to life. As organizations continue to embrace serverless computing and AI, Google Cloud Functions will undoubtedly play a crucial role in shaping the future of technology and driving the next wave of innovation across industries.

Azure Functions: Building AI on Microsoft's Cloud

In the landscape of cloud computing, Azure Functions stands out as a powerful tool for building and deploying serverless applications on Microsoft's Azure cloud platform. With its seamless integration with other Azure services, robust scalability, and support for various programming languages, Azure Functions provides developers with a flexible platform for implementing serverless machine learning (ML) and artificial intelligence (AI) applications. In this article, we'll explore the features and capabilities of Azure Functions, delve into its use cases in serverless ML and AI, and showcase how developers can leverage its power with code examples.

Understanding Azure Functions:

Azure Functions is a serverless compute service provided by Microsoft Azure that enables developers to run code in response to events without provisioning or managing servers. With Azure Functions, developers can upload their code as functions and define triggers to execute them in response to events such as HTTP requests, changes to data in Azure Blob Storage, Cosmos DB, Event Grid events, or timer-based triggers. Azure Functions automatically scales resources to handle incoming requests, ensuring optimal performance and cost-efficiency.

Key Features of Azure Functions:

1. Pay-as-You-Go Pricing: Azure Functions follows a pay-as-you-go pricing model, where developers are charged only for the compute time and resources consumed by their functions, with no upfront costs or minimum fees.

2. Auto-Scaling: Azure Functions automatically scales resources up or down based on workload demands, ensuring that functions have access to the right amount of compute power to handle incoming requests.

3. Integration with Azure Services: Azure Functions seamlessly integrates with other Azure services, allowing developers to build event-driven architectures and automate workflows by connecting functions to services like Azure Blob Storage, Cosmos DB, Event Grid, Azure Service Bus, and more.

4. Multi-Language Support: Azure Functions supports multiple programming languages, including C#, F#, Node.js, Java, PowerShell, Python, and TypeScript, giving developers the flexibility to choose the language that best suits their needs.

Serverless Machine Learning and AI with Azure Functions:

Azure Functions is well-suited for deploying serverless ML and AI applications, offering scalability, cost-efficiency, and seamless integration with other Azure services. Let's explore some common use cases of Azure Functions in serverless ML and AI:

1. Model Inference: Azure Functions can be used to deploy ML models for inference, enabling real-time predictions without managing servers or infrastructure. By integrating Azure Functions with Azure Machine Learning, developers can deploy trained models as serverless functions and invoke them via HTTP endpoints or event triggers.

2. Data Processing: Azure Functions can preprocess data before feeding it into ML models. For example, developers can use Azure Functions to resize images, extract features, or clean and normalize data before training or inference.

3. Chatbots and Natural Language Processing (NLP): Azure Functions can power chatbots and NLP applications, automating customer support, analyzing user feedback, or extracting insights from text data. By integrating Azure Functions with Azure Bot Service or Cognitive Services, developers can build intelligent conversational interfaces that understand and respond to natural language queries.

Example: Image Classification with Azure Functions and Cognitive Services

Let's consider an example of deploying an image classification application using Azure Functions and Azure Cognitive Services:

1. Upload Image to Azure Blob Storage: Users upload images to an Azure Blob Storage container.

2. Trigger Azure Function: An event in Azure Blob Storage triggers an Azure Function, responsible for invoking the Azure Cognitive Services API to analyze and classify the image.

3. Process Image: The Azure Function retrieves the image from Azure Blob Storage, calls the Azure Cognitive Services API to perform image classification, and returns the results.

4. Display Results: The results of the image classification are displayed to the user via a web interface or mobile application.

Code Example: Deploying an Azure Function for Image Classification

Let's write a simple Azure Function using C# to perform image classification with Azure Cognitive Services:

```csharp
using System;
using System.IO;
using System.Threading.Tasks;
using Microsoft.AspNetCore.Mvc;
using Microsoft.Azure.WebJobs;
using Microsoft.Azure.WebJobs.Extensions.Http;
using Microsoft.AspNetCore.Http;
using Microsoft.Extensions.Logging;
using Microsoft.WindowsAzure.Storage.Blob;
using Microsoft.Azure.CognitiveServices.Vision.ComputerVision;
using Microsoft.Azure.CognitiveServices.Vision.ComputerVision.Models;

public static class ImageClassificationFunction
{
    [FunctionName("ClassifyImage")]
    public static async Task<IActionResult> Run(
        [HttpTrigger(AuthorizationLevel.Function, "post", Route = null)] HttpRequest req,
        ILogger log)
    {
```

```csharp
log.LogInformation("C# HTTP trigger function processed a request.");

// Retrieve image data from the request body
var requestBody = await new StreamReader(req.Body).ReadToEndAsync();

// Call the Azure Cognitive Services API to perform image classification
var visionClient = new ComputerVisionClient(new ApiKeyServiceClientCredentials("<YOUR_COGNITIVE_SERVICES_API_KEY>"))
{
    Endpoint = "<YOUR_COGNITIVE_SERVICES_ENDPOINT>"
};

var imageAnalysis = await visionClient.AnalyzeImageAsync(new MemoryStream(Convert.FromBase64String(requestBody)), new List<VisualFeatureTypes> { VisualFeatureTypes.Description });

// Extract and return the image description
return new OkObjectResult(imageAnalysis.Description.Captions.FirstOrDefault().Text);
```

Azure Functions provides developers with a flexible and powerful platform for building and deploying serverless ML and AI applications on Microsoft's Azure cloud platform. With its pay-as-you-go pricing model, auto-scaling capabilities, and seamless integration with other Azure services, Azure Functions enables developers to focus on building innovative solutions without worrying about managing infrastructure. By leveraging Azure Functions, developers can accelerate the pace of innovation and drive the adoption of ML and AI across industries. As Azure Functions continues to evolve, we can expect to see even greater advancements in serverless computing and AI, empowering developers to unlock new possibilities and drive digital transformation on Microsoft's cloud platform.

Choosing the Right Platform for Your Serverless ML and AI Needs

In the rapidly evolving landscape of cloud computing, choosing the right platform for deploying serverless machine learning (ML) and artificial intelligence (AI) applications is crucial for success. With a plethora of options available from various cloud providers, developers need to carefully evaluate factors such as ease of use, scalability, integration capabilities, pricing, and language support. In this article, we'll explore some of the leading cloud platforms for serverless ML and AI, provide code examples, and offer insights to help you make an informed decision.

AWS Lambda: The Power of Amazon's Cloud

AWS Lambda, offered by Amazon Web Services (AWS), is a leading serverless computer service that provides developers with a powerful platform for building and deploying serverless applications. With its seamless integration with other AWS services, robust scalability, and support for multiple programming languages, AWS Lambda is an excellent choice for serverless ML and AI applications.

Code Example:

```python
import boto3

def lambda_handler(event, context):
    # Initialize the Amazon Rekognition client
    rekognition = boto3.client('rekognition')

    # Retrieve the S3 bucket and key from the event
    bucket = event['Records'][0]['s3']['bucket']['name']
```

```
    key = event['Records'][0]['s3']['object']['key']

    # Call the detect_labels API to perform image classification
    response = rekognition.detect_labels(
        Image={
            'S3Object': {
                'Bucket': bucket,
                'Name': key
            },
        },
        MaxLabels=10
    )

    # Extract and return the labels
    labels = [label['Name'] for label in response['Labels']]
    return labels
```
```

## Azure Functions: Microsoft's Cloud Powerhouse

Azure Functions, provided by Microsoft Azure, is another leading serverless compute service that offers developers a flexible platform for deploying serverless applications. With its seamless integration with other Azure services, robust scalability, and support for various programming languages, Azure Functions is a compelling choice for serverless ML and AI applications.
```

Code Example:

```csharp
using System;
using System.IO;
using System.Threading.Tasks;
using Microsoft.AspNetCore.Mvc;
using Microsoft.Azure.WebJobs;
using Microsoft.Azure.WebJobs.Extensions.Http;
using Microsoft.AspNetCore.Http;
using Microsoft.Extensions.Logging;
using Microsoft.WindowsAzure.Storage.Blob;
using Microsoft.Azure.CognitiveServices.Vision.ComputerVision;
using Microsoft.Azure.CognitiveServices.Vision.ComputerVision.Models;

public static class ImageClassificationFunction
{
    [FunctionName("ClassifyImage")]
    public static async Task<IActionResult> Run(
        [HttpTrigger(AuthorizationLevel.Function, "post", Route = null)] HttpRequest req,
        ILogger log)
    {
```

```csharp
log.LogInformation("C# HTTP trigger function processed a request.");

// Retrieve image data from the request body
var requestBody = await new StreamReader(req.Body).ReadToEndAsync();

// Call the Azure Cognitive Services API to perform image classification
var visionClient = new ComputerVisionClient(new ApiKeyServiceClientCredentials("<YOUR_COGNITIVE_SERVICES_API_KEY>"))
{
    Endpoint = "<YOUR_COGNITIVE_SERVICES_ENDPOINT>"
};

var imageAnalysis = await visionClient.AnalyzeImageAsync(new MemoryStream(Convert.FromBase64String(requestBody)), new List<VisualFeatureTypes> { VisualFeatureTypes.Description });

// Extract and return the image description
return new OkObjectResult(imageAnalysis.Description.Captions.FirstOrDefault().Text);
}
```

```

## Google Cloud Functions: The Flexibility of Google's Cloud

Google Cloud Functions, provided by Google Cloud Platform (GCP), is a versatile serverless compute service that offers developers a flexible platform for building and deploying serverless applications. With its seamless integration with other Google Cloud services, robust scalability, and support for multiple programming languages, Google Cloud Functions is a compelling option for serverless ML and AI applications.

**Code Example:**

```python
import base64
from google.cloud import vision

def classify_image(data, context):
    client = vision.ImageAnnotatorClient()

    # Get image data from the Cloud Storage event
    file_data = data['data']
    image_bytes = base64.b64decode(file_data)

    # Perform image classification
```
```

```
image = vision.Image(content=image_bytes)
response = client.label_detection(image=image)
labels = response.label_annotations

# Print labels
for label in labels:
    print(label.description)
```

Choosing the Right Platform:

When choosing the right platform for your serverless ML and AI needs, consider the following factors:

1. Integration: Evaluate how well the platform integrates with other services and tools you use in your workflow.

2. Scalability: Ensure that the platform can scale seamlessly to handle your application's workload demands.

3. Pricing: Compare the pricing models of different platforms to find the most cost-effective option for your budget.

4. Language Support: Choose a platform that supports the programming languages you are comfortable with and that best suit your application's requirements.

By carefully evaluating these factors and experimenting with code examples, you can choose the right platform for your serverless ML and AI needs and build intelligent applications with ease. Whether you opt for AWS Lambda, Azure Functions, Google Cloud Functions, or another platform, you'll find a powerful and flexible environment to bring your ideas to life.

Chapter 4

Serverless Frameworks: Simplifying Development (e.g., Serverless Framework, AWS SAM)

Serverless computing has revolutionized the way developers build and deploy applications, offering a cost-effective and scalable solution for various use cases, including machine learning (ML) and artificial intelligence (AI). To streamline the development and deployment process, serverless frameworks such as Serverless Framework and AWS SAM (Serverless Application Model) have emerged as powerful tools. In this article, we'll explore these frameworks, discuss their features, and demonstrate how they simplify the development of serverless ML and AI applications with code examples.

Introducing Serverless Framework:

Serverless Framework is an open-source framework that provides developers with a simple and consistent way to build, deploy, and manage serverless applications across different cloud providers. With support for multiple programming languages and extensive integrations with various cloud services, Serverless Framework simplifies the development process and reduces the time and effort required to deploy serverless applications.

Key Features of Serverless Framework:

1. Multi-Cloud Support: Serverless Framework supports multiple cloud providers, including AWS, Azure, Google Cloud Platform, and more, allowing developers to deploy applications to their preferred cloud environment seamlessly.

2. Infrastructure as Code (IaC): Serverless Framework enables developers to define their application infrastructure as code using YAML or JSON, making it easy to version control, share, and replicate deployments.

3. Plugin Ecosystem: Serverless Framework boasts a rich ecosystem of plugins that extend its functionality, providing additional features and integrations with third-party services, such as monitoring, logging, and security.

4. Local Development: Serverless Framework provides tools for local development and testing, allowing developers to simulate serverless environments on their local machines before deploying applications to the cloud.

AWS SAM: Serverless Application Model

AWS SAM (Serverless Application Model) is an open-source framework provided by Amazon Web Services (AWS) for building serverless applications on AWS cloud infrastructure. Built on top of AWS CloudFormation, SAM simplifies the process of defining and deploying serverless applications on AWS, providing developers with a streamlined workflow and integration with AWS services.

Key Features of AWS SAM:

1. Declarative Syntax: AWS SAM uses a declarative YAML syntax to define serverless applications, making it easy to describe resources such as functions, APIs, and event sources in a human-readable format.

2. Local Testing: AWS SAM provides tools for local testing and debugging of serverless applications, allowing developers to iterate quickly and troubleshoot issues before deploying to AWS cloud.

3. Built-in Resources: AWS SAM includes built-in resources for common serverless use cases, such as API Gateway, Lambda functions, DynamoDB tables, and more, reducing the need for manual configuration.

4. Integration with AWS Services: AWS SAM seamlessly integrates with other AWS services, enabling developers to leverage the full power of the AWS ecosystem for building and deploying serverless applications.

Simplifying Development with Serverless Frameworks:

Let's explore how Serverless Framework and AWS SAM simplify the development of serverless ML and AI applications with code examples:

Example: Deploying a Serverless ML Model with Serverless Framework

```yaml
# serverless.yml
service: my-ml-service

provider:
  name: aws
  runtime: python3.8

functions:
  predict:
    handler: predict.handler
    events:
```

```
      - http:
          path: predict
          method: post
```

```python
# predict.py
import json

def handler(event, context):
    # Load ML model
    # Perform prediction
    # Return result
    return {
        "statusCode": 200,
        "body": json.dumps({"prediction": "label"})
    }
```

Example: Deploying a Serverless NLP Application with AWS SAM

```yaml
# template.yaml
AWSTemplateFormatVersion: '2010-09-09'
Transform: 'AWS::Serverless-2016-10-31'

Resources:
  MyFunction:
```

```yaml
      Type: 'AWS::Serverless::Function'
      Properties:
        Handler: handler.handler
        Runtime: python3.8
        Events:
          MyEvent:
            Type: Api
            Properties:
              Path: /nlp
              Method: post
```

```python
# handler.py
import json

def handler(event, context):
    # Process NLP request
    # Return result
    return {
        "statusCode": 200,
        "body": json.dumps({"result": "processed"})
    }
```

Serverless frameworks such as Serverless Framework and AWS SAM simplify the development and deployment of serverless ML and AI applications by providing streamlined workflows, infrastructure as code capabilities, and integration with cloud services. Whether you're deploying ML models for inference, building NLP applications, or developing intelligent chatbots, these frameworks offer the tools and resources you need to bring your ideas to life quickly and efficiently. By leveraging the power of serverless computing and these frameworks, developers can focus on building innovative solutions without worrying about managing infrastructure, ultimately driving the adoption of ML and AI across industries.

Machine Learning Frameworks in the Serverless World (e.g., TensorFlow, PyTorch)

Machine learning (ML) frameworks play a crucial role in building and deploying intelligent applications in the serverless world. With the advent of serverless computing, developers can leverage the scalability and cost-efficiency of cloud platforms while harnessing the power of ML frameworks to train models and perform inference tasks. In this article, we'll explore popular ML frameworks such as TensorFlow and PyTorch, discuss their integration with serverless platforms, and provide code examples to demonstrate how they enable serverless ML and AI.

TensorFlow: Powering Serverless Machine Learning

TensorFlow, developed by Google, is one of the most widely used open-source ML frameworks, known for its flexibility, scalability, and extensive ecosystem of tools and libraries. With TensorFlow, developers can build and train various types of ML models, including neural networks, deep learning models, and reinforcement learning algorithms. In the serverless world, TensorFlow enables developers to deploy ML models as serverless functions, perform inference tasks, and integrate with cloud services seamlessly.

Integration with Serverless Platforms:

TensorFlow can be integrated with serverless platforms such as AWS Lambda, Azure Functions, and Google Cloud Functions to deploy ML models for inference tasks. Developers can package trained TensorFlow models along with their serverless functions and invoke them via HTTP endpoints or event triggers. Additionally, TensorFlow Serving, a dedicated serving system for deploying ML models in production environments, can be deployed as a serverless function to handle model inference requests at scale.

Example: Deploying a TensorFlow Model on AWS Lambda

```python
```

```python
import tensorflow as tf

def handler(event, context):
    # Load TensorFlow model
    model = tf.keras.models.load_model('model.h5')

    # Perform inference
    input_data = event['data']
    predictions = model.predict(input_data)

    # Return predictions
    return {
        "statusCode": 200,
        "body": {"predictions": predictions}
    }
```

PyTorch: Flexibility and Performance in Serverless ML

PyTorch, developed by Facebook, is another popular ML framework known for its dynamic computation graph, ease of use, and strong community support. PyTorch is widely used for building and training deep learning models, including convolutional neural networks (CNNs), recurrent neural networks (RNNs), and transformers. In the serverless world, PyTorch enables developers to deploy and run ML models as serverless functions, leveraging its flexibility and performance advantages.

Integration with Serverless Platforms:

Similar to TensorFlow, PyTorch can be integrated with serverless platforms to deploy ML models for inference tasks. Developers can package trained PyTorch models along with their serverless functions and deploy them on platforms like AWS Lambda, Azure Functions, and Google Cloud Functions. Additionally, PyTorch's TorchServe, a flexible and easy-to-use model serving library, can be deployed as a serverless function to handle inference requests efficiently.

Example: Deploying a PyTorch Model on Azure Functions

```python
import torch
import torchvision.transforms as transforms
from PIL import Image

def handler(event, context):
    # Load PyTorch model
    model = torch.load('model.pth')
    model.eval()
```

```python
# Preprocess input data
input_image = Image.open(event['image'])
preprocess = transforms.Compose([
    transforms.Resize(256),
    transforms.CenterCrop(224),
    transforms.ToTensor(),
    transforms.Normalize(mean=[0.485, 0.456, 0.406], std=[0.229, 0.224, 0.225]),
])
input_tensor = preprocess(input_image)
input_batch = input_tensor.unsqueeze(0)

# Perform inference
with torch.no_grad():
    output = model(input_batch)

# Return predictions
return {
    "statusCode": 200,
    "body": {"predictions": output}
}
```
```

Machine learning frameworks such as TensorFlow and PyTorch empower developers to build and deploy intelligent applications in the serverless world, leveraging the scalability and flexibility of cloud platforms. By integrating these frameworks with
```

serverless platforms, developers can deploy ML models as serverless functions, perform inference tasks, and handle prediction requests at scale. Whether you're deploying image classification models, natural language processing (NLP) models, or recommendation systems, TensorFlow and PyTorch provide the tools and capabilities you need to succeed in the serverless ML and AI landscape. With the convergence of serverless computing and machine learning, the possibilities for building intelligent applications are endless, and these frameworks serve as the foundation for innovation and progress in the field.

Model Deployment and Management Services (e.g., Amazon SageMaker, Google AI Platform)

Model deployment and management are critical aspects of building and deploying machine learning (ML) and artificial intelligence (AI) applications. With the rise of serverless computing, developers now have access to managed services that simplify the deployment and management of ML models on cloud platforms. In this article, we'll explore two leading model deployment and management services: Amazon SageMaker and Google AI Platform. We'll discuss their features, integration with serverless platforms, and provide code examples to demonstrate how they enable serverless ML and AI.

Amazon SageMaker: Streamlining ML Model Deployment

Amazon SageMaker, provided by Amazon Web Services (AWS), is a fully managed service that enables developers to build, train, and deploy ML models at scale. SageMaker offers a comprehensive set of tools and capabilities for every step of the ML workflow, from data preparation and model training to deployment and monitoring. With SageMaker, developers can easily deploy trained models as RESTful APIs, perform batch inference, and monitor model performance in real-time.

Key Features of Amazon SageMaker:

1. Built-in Algorithms: SageMaker provides a collection of built-in ML algorithms and pre-built models for common use cases, making it easy to get started with model training and experimentation.

2. Managed Training: SageMaker automates the process of training ML models by provisioning and managing the underlying infrastructure, enabling developers to focus on model development rather than infrastructure management.

3. Model Deployment: SageMaker offers seamless deployment options for ML models, including deploying models as real-time endpoints, batch transforms, or serverless functions using AWS Lambda.

4. Model Monitoring: SageMaker provides built-in monitoring capabilities to track model performance, detect drift, and generate alerts when anomalies are detected, ensuring that deployed models remain accurate and reliable over time.

Integration with Serverless Platforms:

SageMaker can be integrated with serverless platforms such as AWS Lambda to deploy ML models as serverless functions. Developers can use SageMaker's deployment capabilities to package trained models as Docker containers and deploy them as Lambda functions, enabling scalable and cost-effective model inference without managing infrastructure.

Example: Deploying a SageMaker Model on AWS Lambda

```python
import boto3
import json

def handler(event, context):
    # Load SageMaker model
```

```
client = boto3.client('sagemaker-runtime')
response = client.invoke_endpoint(
    EndpointName='my-endpoint',
    ContentType='application/json',
    Body=json.dumps(event['data'])
)

# Parse and return predictions
predictions = json.loads(response['Body'].read().decode())
return {
    "statusCode": 200,
    "body": {"predictions": predictions}
}
```

Google AI Platform: Simplifying ML Model Management

Google AI Platform, provided by Google Cloud Platform (GCP), is a managed service that enables developers to build, train, and deploy ML models on Google Cloud. AI Platform offers a suite of tools and services for ML model management, including model training, hyperparameter tuning, and model serving. With AI Platform, developers can deploy trained models as scalable and reliable APIs, making it easy to integrate ML capabilities into applications.

Key Features of Google AI Platform:

1. Unified ML Platform: AI Platform provides a unified platform for ML model development, training, deployment, and monitoring, streamlining the end-to-end ML workflow.

2. Hyperparameter Tuning: AI Platform offers built-in support for hyperparameter tuning, allowing developers to optimize model performance and achieve better results with less manual effort.

3. Model Versioning: AI Platform supports model versioning, enabling developers to manage and track multiple versions of ML models, compare performance metrics, and roll back to previous versions if needed.

4. Model Monitoring and Debugging: AI Platform provides tools for monitoring model performance, detecting anomalies, and debugging issues in real-time, ensuring that deployed models meet performance requirements.

Integration with Serverless Platforms:

AI Platform can be integrated with serverless platforms such as Google Cloud Functions to deploy ML models as serverless functions. Developers can use AI Platform's model deployment capabilities to expose trained models as HTTP endpoints, enabling scalable and cost-effective model inference without managing infrastructure.

Example: Deploying an AI Platform Model on Google Cloud Functions

```python
from google.cloud import aiplatform

def handler(request):
    # Load AI Platform model
    model = aiplatform.ModelEndpoint(endpoint="my-endpoint")

    # Perform inference
    input_data = request.get_json()
    response = model.predict(instances=input_data)

    # Return predictions
    return response
```

Model deployment and management services such as Amazon SageMaker and Google AI Platform play a crucial role in simplifying the deployment and management of ML models in the serverless world. By leveraging these managed services, developers can streamline the ML workflow, deploy models at scale, and integrate ML capabilities into their applications with ease. Whether you choose SageMaker or AI Platform, you'll find a powerful and flexible environment to deploy and manage ML models in the serverless world, enabling you to unlock the full potential of machine learning and artificial intelligence.

Integrating with APIs and Data Sources: Building the AI Ecosystem

In the realm of artificial intelligence (AI) and machine learning (ML), access to diverse data sources and external APIs is crucial for building robust and intelligent applications. With the advent of serverless computing, developers now have powerful tools and platforms to seamlessly integrate with APIs and data sources, enabling them to build a rich AI ecosystem. In this article, we'll explore the importance of integrating with APIs and data sources in the context of serverless ML and AI, discuss common use cases, and provide code examples to demonstrate how to leverage these integrations effectively.

Importance of Integration with APIs and Data Sources:

Integrating with external APIs and data sources opens up a world of possibilities for AI and ML applications. By accessing diverse datasets and external services, developers can enhance the capabilities of their AI models, improve accuracy, and provide more valuable insights to users. Whether it's integrating with social media APIs for sentiment analysis, accessing weather data for predictive modeling, or leveraging third-party services for image recognition, APIs and data sources play a crucial role in building the AI ecosystem.

Common Use Cases for Integration:

1. Data Enrichment: Integrating with external data sources allows developers to enrich their datasets with additional information, such as demographic data, geographic data, or industry-specific data, enhancing the quality and relevance of AI models.

2. Real-time Data Processing: APIs provide access to real-time data streams from various sources, enabling developers to perform real-time analysis, monitoring, and decision-making in AI applications.

3. Content Analysis: Integrating with natural language processing (NLP) APIs allows developers to analyze text data, extract entities, perform sentiment analysis, and generate insights from unstructured text sources such as social media, news articles, or customer reviews.

4. Image Recognition: Integrating with image recognition APIs enables developers to analyze and classify images, detect objects, and extract information from visual content, enhancing the capabilities of AI models in image-based applications.

Integration with Serverless Platforms:

Serverless platforms such as AWS Lambda, Azure Functions, and Google Cloud Functions provide an ideal environment for integrating with APIs and data sources. By deploying serverless functions, developers can easily access external APIs, process data in real-time, and integrate with cloud-based data storage services, all without managing infrastructure or provisioning servers.

Code Examples:

Let's explore a few code examples to demonstrate how to integrate with APIs and data sources in a serverless environment:

Example 1: Integrating with Twitter API for Sentiment Analysis

```python
import tweepy
from textblob import TextBlob

def analyze_tweet(tweet):
    analysis = TextBlob(tweet)
    return analysis.sentiment.polarity

def handler(event, context):
    # Authenticate with Twitter API
    auth = tweepy.OAuthHandler(consumer_key, consumer_secret)
    auth.set_access_token(access_token, access_token_secret)
    api = tweepy.API(auth)

    # Fetch tweets
    tweets = api.search(q=event['query'], count=event['count'])

    # Perform sentiment analysis
    sentiments = [analyze_tweet(tweet.text) for tweet in tweets]

    # Return sentiment scores
    return {
        "statusCode": 200,
        "body": {"sentiments": sentiments}
```

    }
```

## Example 2: Integrating with OpenWeatherMap API for Weather Data

```python
import requests

def fetch_weather(city):
    url = f"http://api.openweathermap.org/data/2.5/weather?q={city}&appid={api_key}"
    response = requests.get(url)
    data = response.json()
    return data['main']['temp']

def handler(event, context):
    # Fetch weather data
    temperature = fetch_weather(event['city'])

    # Return temperature
    return {
        "statusCode": 200,
        "body": {"temperature": temperature}
    }
```
```

Integrating with APIs and data sources is essential for building a rich AI ecosystem and enhancing the capabilities of ML and AI applications. In the serverless world, developers can leverage the scalability, flexibility, and cost-efficiency of serverless platforms to seamlessly integrate with external services and access diverse datasets in real-time. By leveraging APIs and data sources effectively, developers can unlock new possibilities, improve the accuracy of AI models, and deliver more valuable insights to users, ultimately driving innovation and progress in the field of artificial intelligence.

Chapter 5

Hands-On with Serverless AI: A Step-by-Step Guide

Choosing Your AI Project: Solving Real-World Problems

Artificial intelligence (AI) has become increasingly accessible to developers thanks to advancements in cloud computing and serverless technology. In this step-by-step guide, we'll walk through the process of building a serverless AI project from start to finish. We'll start by choosing a real-world problem to solve, then dive into the implementation details using serverless machine learning and AI techniques. Let's get started!

Step 1: Choosing Your AI Project

Before diving into implementation, it's crucial to choose a real-world problem that can be solved using AI. Here are a few examples of potential AI projects:

1. Image Classification: Build an AI model to classify images into different categories, such as identifying different types of animals or recognizing objects in images.

2. Sentiment Analysis: Develop an AI model to analyze the sentiment of text data, such as social media posts or customer reviews, to determine whether the sentiment is positive, negative, or neutral.

3. Predictive Maintenance: Create an AI model to predict when equipment or machinery is likely to fail based on historical data, enabling proactive maintenance and reducing downtime.

4. Natural Language Processing (NLP): Build an AI model to perform tasks such as language translation, text summarization, or named entity recognition, to extract insights from unstructured text data.

Once you've chosen your AI project, you can proceed to the implementation phase using serverless machine learning and AI techniques.

Step 2: Implementation with Serverless Technology

For the purpose of this guide, let's choose the project of building an AI model for sentiment analysis of social media posts. We'll use serverless technology to deploy our model and perform inference in real-time. Here's a step-by-step guide to the implementation:

1. Data Collection:

- Gather a dataset of social media posts along with their associated sentiment labels (positive, negative, neutral).

- You can use public datasets or collect your own data using APIs from social media platforms.

2. Data Preprocessing:

- Clean and preprocess the text data by removing noise, punctuation, and stopwords.

- Convert text data into a numerical format suitable for training an AI model, such as word embeddings or TF-IDF vectors.

3. Model Training:

- Choose an appropriate machine learning or deep learning model for sentiment analysis, such as a recurrent neural network (RNN) or a transformer-based model like BERT.

- Train the model using the preprocessed data, optimizing it for sentiment classification.

4. Model Deployment:

- Deploy the trained model as a serverless function using a platform like AWS Lambda, Azure Functions, or Google Cloud Functions.

- Expose the model as a RESTful API endpoint, allowing users to submit text data for sentiment analysis.

5. Inference and Result Presentation:

- Receive incoming requests containing text data to be analyzed for sentiment.

- Perform inference using the deployed serverless model, predicting the sentiment of the text data.

- Return the predicted sentiment (positive, negative, neutral) as the result of the API call.

Example Code (Python with AWS Lambda):

```python
import boto3
from textblob import TextBlob

def analyze_sentiment(text):
    analysis = TextBlob(text)
```

```
    if analysis.sentiment.polarity > 0:
        return "positive"
    elif analysis.sentiment.polarity < 0:
        return "negative"
    else:
        return "neutral"

def lambda_handler(event, context):
    text = event['text']
    sentiment = analyze_sentiment(text)
    return {
        "statusCode": 200,
        "body": {"sentiment": sentiment}
    }
```

In this hands-on guide, we've walked through the process of choosing an AI project, implementing it using serverless technology, and deploying it as a serverless function. By following these steps, you can build and deploy your own serverless AI projects to solve real-world problems efficiently and cost-effectively. Remember to choose a project that aligns with your interests and expertise, and don't hesitate to experiment with different AI techniques and serverless platforms to achieve the best results. Happy coding!

Designing Your Serverless AI Architecture: Breaking Down the Workflow

Designing a serverless architecture for AI applications involves breaking down the workflow into smaller components, each responsible for a specific task. In this guide, we'll explore the key components of a serverless AI architecture, discuss best practices for designing scalable and efficient systems, and provide code examples to illustrate the implementation. Let's dive in!

Key Components of a Serverless AI Architecture

1. Data Ingestion: The first step in any AI workflow is to ingest data from various sources, such as databases, data lakes, or streaming platforms. In a serverless architecture, you can use services like AWS S3, Azure Blob Storage, or Google Cloud Storage to store and manage your data.

2. Data Preprocessing: Once the data is ingested, it needs to be cleaned, transformed, and prepared for model training. Serverless functions can be used to preprocess data in parallel, enabling scalable and efficient processing. For example, you can use AWS Lambda, Azure Functions, or Google Cloud Functions for data preprocessing tasks.

3. Model Training: After preprocessing, the data is used to train machine learning models. In a serverless architecture, you can leverage managed ML services like Amazon SageMaker, Azure Machine Learning, or Google AI Platform for model training. These services handle the underlying infrastructure, allowing you to focus on model development.

4. Model Deployment: Once the model is trained, it needs to be deployed to production for inference. Serverless functions can be used to deploy ML models as RESTful APIs, enabling real-time inference on incoming data. For example, you can deploy models using AWS Lambda, Azure Functions, or Google Cloud Functions.

5. Inference and Result Presentation: In the final step of the workflow, incoming data is sent to the deployed model for inference. The model predicts the output, which is then presented to the user or stored for further analysis. Serverless functions handle incoming requests, perform inference, and return the results to the user.

Best Practices for Designing a Serverless AI Architecture

1. Decoupling Components: Design your architecture to be modular and decoupled, with each component responsible for a specific task. This allows for easier maintenance, scalability, and flexibility.

2. Asynchronous Processing: Use asynchronous processing whenever possible to improve performance and scalability. For example, use message queues or event-driven architectures to decouple components and handle bursts of incoming data.

3. Optimized Resource Usage: Optimize resource usage by leveraging serverless functions for short-lived, compute-intensive tasks. This reduces costs and improves scalability by only paying for the resources used during execution.

4. Monitoring and Logging: Implement monitoring and logging to track the performance of your serverless functions and detect issues in real-time. Use services like AWS CloudWatch, Azure Monitor, or Google Cloud Logging to monitor function invocations, errors, and resource usage.

Example Code (Python with AWS Lambda):

```python
import boto3
from sklearn.externals import joblib
```

```
def predict(event, context):
    # Load trained model from S3
    s3 = boto3.client('s3')
    s3.download_file('my-bucket', 'model.pkl', '/tmp/model.pkl')
    model = joblib.load('/tmp/model.pkl')

    # Preprocess input data
    data = preprocess(event['data'])

    # Perform inference
    prediction = model.predict(data)

    # Return prediction
    return {
        "statusCode": 200,
        "body": {"prediction": prediction}
    }
```

Designing a serverless AI architecture involves breaking down the workflow into smaller, modular components and leveraging serverless technologies to achieve scalability, efficiency, and cost-effectiveness. By following best practices and utilizing managed services for data processing, model training, and inference, you can build robust and scalable AI systems that meet the needs of your organization. Experiment with different architectures, services, and tools to find the best fit for your specific use case, and continue to iterate and improve as needed. With the right design and implementation, you can unleash the full potential of serverless AI and drive innovation in your organization.

Coding Your Serverless AI Hero: Putting the Pieces Together

Bringing your serverless AI architecture to life involves coding the various components and putting them together to create a cohesive system. In this guide, we'll walk through the process of coding a serverless AI solution, from data preprocessing to model deployment, and provide code examples using serverless technologies. Let's dive in and build our serverless AI hero!

Step 1: Data Preprocessing

Data preprocessing is a critical step in the AI workflow, involving cleaning, transforming, and preparing the data for model training. Let's create a serverless function to preprocess our data using AWS Lambda and Python.

```python
import pandas as pd
import numpy as np
```

```
def preprocess_data(event, context):
    # Load data from S3
    data = pd.read_csv('s3://my-bucket/data.csv')

    # Perform preprocessing steps
    # Example: Remove missing values
    data = data.dropna()

    # Convert categorical variables to numerical
    data['category'] = pd.factorize(data['category'])[0]

    # Convert data to numpy array
    X = data.drop('target', axis=1).values
    y = data['target'].values

    return X, y
```

Step 2: Model Training

Once the data is preprocessed, we can train our machine learning model using a serverless approach. Let's train a simple logistic regression model using scikit-learn and AWS Lambda.

```python
from sklearn.linear_model import LogisticRegression
```

```python
def train_model(event, context):
    # Preprocess data
    X, y = preprocess_data(event, context)

    # Train model
    model = LogisticRegression()
    model.fit(X, y)

    # Serialize and save model
    joblib.dump(model, '/tmp/model.pkl')

    return 'Model trained and saved successfully!'
```

Step 3: Model Deployment

With our model trained, it's time to deploy it as a serverless function for inference. We'll use AWS Lambda to deploy our model and expose it as a RESTful API endpoint.

```python
import joblib

def predict(event, context):
    # Load trained model
    model = joblib.load('/tmp/model.pkl')
```

```
# Preprocess input data
data = preprocess_input(event['data'])

# Perform inference
prediction = model.predict(data)

return {
    "statusCode": 200,
    "body": {"prediction": prediction.tolist()}
}
```

Step 4: Integration and Testing

Now that we have our serverless functions coded, we can integrate them together and test the end-to-end workflow. We'll invoke the preprocessing function to preprocess our input data, then pass the preprocessed data to the model prediction function for inference.

```python
import json
import boto3

# Initialize AWS Lambda client
lambda_client = boto3.client('lambda')

# Input data for testing
```

```python
input_data = {
    "data": [1.5, 2.0, 3.5]
}

# Invoke preprocessing function
preprocessing_response = lambda_client.invoke(
    FunctionName='preprocess_data',
    InvocationType='RequestResponse',
    Payload=json.dumps(input_data)
)

# Parse preprocessing response
preprocessed_data = json.loads(preprocessing_response['Payload'].read())

# Invoke model prediction function
prediction_response = lambda_client.invoke(
    FunctionName='predict',
    InvocationType='RequestResponse',
    Payload=json.dumps({"data": preprocessed_data})
)

# Parse prediction response
prediction_result = json.loads(prediction_response['Payload'].read())
print(prediction_result)
```
```
```

Coding your serverless AI hero involves breaking down the AI workflow into smaller, manageable components and implementing them using serverless technologies such as AWS Lambda, Azure Functions, or Google Cloud Functions. By following the steps outlined in this guide and leveraging serverless platforms, you can build scalable, efficient, and cost-effective AI solutions that meet the needs of your organization. Experiment with different algorithms, architectures, and deployment strategies to find the best fit for your specific use case, and continue to iterate and improve as needed. With the right coding and implementation, you can unleash the full potential of serverless AI and drive innovation in your organization.

Deploying Your AI Application: Unleashing Your Serverless Masterpiece

Deploying your AI application is the final step in the journey of bringing your serverless masterpiece to life. In this guide, we'll explore the process of deploying your serverless AI application, including packaging and deploying your model, setting up API endpoints, and ensuring scalability and reliability. We'll provide code examples using serverless technologies to illustrate each step of the deployment process. Let's dive in and unleash your serverless masterpiece!

Step 1: Package and Deploy Your Model

The first step in deploying your AI application is to package your trained model and deploy it to a serverless environment. Let's use AWS Lambda as an example and deploy a trained model using a Lambda function.

```python
import boto3
import joblib

def deploy_model(event, context):
    # Load trained model
    model = joblib.load('model.pkl')

    # Serialize model and upload to S3
    s3 = boto3.client('s3')
    s3.put_object(Body=model, Bucket='my-bucket', Key='model.pkl')

    return 'Model deployed successfully!'
```

Step 2: Set Up API Endpoints

Once your model is deployed, you'll need to set up API endpoints to expose your AI functionality to users or other applications. You can use API Gateway in conjunction with AWS Lambda to create RESTful APIs for your AI application.

```python
import json

def predict(event, context):
    # Load model from S3
    s3 = boto3.client('s3')
    model = joblib.load(s3.get_object(Bucket='my-bucket', Key='model.pkl')['Body'])

    # Perform inference
    data = json.loads(event['body'])
    prediction = model.predict(data)

    # Return prediction
    return {
        "statusCode": 200,
        "body": json.dumps({"prediction": prediction.tolist()})
    }
```

Step 3: Deploy Your API

With your API endpoints defined, it's time to deploy your API to a serverless environment. You can use AWS

API Gateway to create and deploy your API, making it accessible to users or other applications.

```python
import boto3

def deploy_api(event, context):
    # Deploy API using AWS API Gateway
    apigateway = boto3.client('apigateway')
    response = apigateway.create_deployment(
        restApiId='my-api-id',
        stageName='prod'
    )

    return 'API deployed successfully!'
```

Step 4: Testing and Scaling

Before unleashing your AI application to the world, it's essential to test it thoroughly and ensure scalability and reliability. You can use tools like AWS CloudFormation to automate the deployment process and AWS CloudWatch to monitor the performance of your serverless functions and API endpoints.

```python
import boto3
```

```
def scale(event, context):
    # Automatically scale AWS Lambda function
    lambda_client = boto3.client('lambda')
    response = lambda_client.update_function_configuration(
        FunctionName='my-function-name',
        MemorySize=2048
    )

    return 'Function scaled successfully!'
```

Deploying your AI application is an exciting milestone in your journey of building and unleashing your serverless masterpiece. By following the steps outlined in this guide and leveraging serverless technologies such as AWS Lambda, API Gateway, and S3, you can deploy your AI application with ease and confidence. Experiment with different deployment strategies, monitor performance, and scale as needed to meet the demands of your users or customers. With the power of serverless computing and AI, the possibilities are endless, and you have the tools and technologies at your disposal to create innovative and impactful AI applications that drive value for your organization.

Chapter 6

Common Serverless AI Use Cases and Applications

Image Recognition: Seeing the World Through AI's Eyes

Image recognition, a subset of computer vision, enables machines to interpret and understand the content of images. With advancements in artificial intelligence (AI) and machine learning (ML), image recognition has become increasingly accurate and efficient, opening up a wide range of applications across industries. In this guide, we'll explore the fascinating world of image recognition, discuss its principles and techniques, and provide code examples using serverless machine learning and AI.

Understanding Image Recognition

Image recognition involves teaching computers to recognize objects, patterns, and features within images. It relies on deep learning algorithms, such as convolutional neural networks (CNNs), which are specifically designed to analyze visual data. These algorithms learn to identify objects by extracting features from images and mapping them to predefined categories or labels.

Key Techniques in Image Recognition

1. Convolutional Neural Networks (CNNs): CNNs are the backbone of modern image recognition systems. They consist of multiple layers of convolutional and pooling operations, followed by fully connected layers for classification. CNNs can automatically learn hierarchical features from raw image data, making them highly effective for image recognition tasks.

2. Transfer Learning: Transfer learning is a technique that leverages pre-trained CNN models, such as ResNet, VGG, or Inception, and fine-tunes them for specific image recognition tasks. This approach allows developers to achieve high accuracy with less training data and computational resources.

3. Data Augmentation: Data augmentation involves generating additional training data by applying transformations, such as rotation, scaling, and flipping, to existing images. This technique helps improve the robustness and generalization of image recognition models by exposing them to a wider range of variations in the input data.

Implementing Image Recognition with Serverless Technology

Now, let's dive into implementing image recognition using serverless machine learning and AI. We'll use AWS Lambda and a pre-trained image recognition model to classify images uploaded to an S3 bucket.

```python
import boto3
from PIL import Image
import numpy as np
from tensorflow.keras.applications.resnet50 import ResNet50, preprocess_input, decode_predictions

# Load pre-trained ResNet50 model
model = ResNet50(weights='imagenet')

def classify_image(event, context):
    # Get S3 bucket and key from event
    bucket = event['Records'][0]['s3']['bucket']['name']
    key = event['Records'][0]['s3']['object']['key']

    # Download image from S3
    s3 = boto3.client('s3')
    response = s3.get_object(Bucket=bucket, Key=key)
    image = Image.open(response['Body'])

    # Preprocess image
    image = image.resize((224, 224))
```

```
    image = np.array(image)
    image = preprocess_input(image)
    image = np.expand_dims(image, axis=0)

    # Perform inference
    predictions = model.predict(image)
    decoded_predictions = decode_predictions(predictions, top=3)[0]

    # Return top 3 predictions
    return {
        "statusCode": 200,
        "body": {"predictions": decoded_predictions}
    }
```

Image recognition enables machines to interpret and understand visual data, opening up a wide range of possibilities across industries, from healthcare and agriculture to retail and manufacturing. By leveraging serverless machine learning and AI, developers can implement image recognition solutions that are scalable, efficient, and cost-effective. Experiment with different pre-trained models, fine-tuning techniques, and serverless platforms to build innovative image recognition applications that see the world through AI's eyes. With the power of image recognition and serverless technology, the future of visual intelligence is limitless.

Chatbots and Virtual Assistants: Powering Intelligent Conversations

Chatbots and virtual assistants have become integral parts of our daily lives, revolutionizing how we interact with technology and access information. These AI-powered conversational interfaces enable seamless communication between users and machines, providing assistance, answering questions, and performing tasks in natural language. In this guide, we'll delve into the world of chatbots and virtual assistants, explore the underlying technologies and techniques, and provide code examples using serverless machine learning and artificial intelligence.

Understanding Chatbots and Virtual Assistants

Chatbots and virtual assistants are AI-driven applications designed to simulate human-like conversation and provide assistance to users. They leverage natural language processing (NLP), machine learning, and other AI techniques to understand user queries, generate responses, and perform actions. Chatbots can be deployed across various platforms, including websites, messaging apps, and voice assistants, making them versatile tools for engaging with users in different contexts.

Key Technologies and Techniques

1. Natural Language Processing (NLP): NLP enables chatbots to understand and interpret human language, including speech and text. NLP techniques such as tokenization, named entity recognition, and sentiment analysis are used to analyze and process user input, extract relevant information, and generate appropriate responses.

2. Machine Learning: Machine learning algorithms, such as recurrent neural networks (RNNs) and transformers, are used to train chatbots on large datasets of conversational data. These algorithms learn to generate contextually relevant responses based on patterns in the training data, improving the conversational capabilities of chatbots over time.

3. Dialog Management: Dialog management techniques are used to structure and manage conversations between users and chatbots. Dialog managers keep track of context, handle multi-turn conversations, and guide the flow of the conversation to achieve the desired outcome.

Implementing Chatbots with Serverless Technology

Let's dive into implementing a simple chatbot using serverless machine learning and AI. We'll use AWS Lambda and the ChatterBot library to create a basic chatbot that responds to user queries with predefined responses.

```python
from chatterbot import ChatBot
from chatterbot.trainers import ChatterBotCorpusTrainer

# Create chatbot instance
chatbot = ChatBot('MyChatBot')

# Train chatbot on English corpus
trainer = ChatterBotCorpusTrainer(chatbot)
trainer.train('chatterbot.corpus.english')

def respond_to_message(event, context):
    # Get user message from event
    user_message = event['message']

    # Get chatbot response
    response = chatbot.get_response(user_message)

    return {
        "statusCode": 200,
        "body": {"response": str(response)}
```

}
```

Chatbots and virtual assistants are transforming how we interact with technology, enabling intelligent conversations and providing personalized assistance to users across various platforms. By leveraging serverless machine learning and AI, developers can build chatbots that are scalable, efficient, and cost-effective. Experiment with different NLP techniques, machine learning algorithms, and serverless platforms to create innovative chatbot solutions that power intelligent conversations and enhance user experiences. With the power of chatbots and virtual assistants, the future of human-computer interaction is bright and full of possibilities.

## Fraud Detection: Keeping Your Business Safe from Bad Actors

Fraud detection is a critical aspect of safeguarding any business, especially in today's digital landscape where bad actors are constantly devising new ways to exploit vulnerabilities. Leveraging serverless machine learning and artificial intelligence (AI) technologies can significantly enhance a company's ability to detect and prevent fraudulent activities in real-time. In this comprehensive guide, we'll explore how businesses can
```

utilize these advanced techniques to protect themselves against fraudsters.

Introduction to Fraud Detection

Fraud can take various forms, including payment fraud, identity theft, account takeover, and more. Regardless of the type, the consequences of fraud can be devastating for businesses, leading to financial losses, damaged reputation, and legal implications. Therefore, implementing robust fraud detection mechanisms is essential for mitigating these risks.

The Role of Machine Learning and AI

Machine learning and AI algorithms play a pivotal role in fraud detection by analyzing large volumes of data to identify patterns and anomalies indicative of fraudulent behavior. By continuously learning from new data, these algorithms can adapt to evolving fraud tactics, making them highly effective in combating fraud in real-time.

Serverless Architecture for Scalability and Flexibility

Serverless architecture offers scalability and flexibility, making it an ideal choice for implementing fraud detection systems. With serverless computing, resources are provisioned dynamically, allowing applications to scale automatically in response to changes in demand. This ensures that fraud detection systems can handle fluctuating workloads efficiently without the need for manual intervention.

Building a Serverless Fraud Detection System

Let's outline the steps involved in building a serverless fraud detection system using machine learning and AI:

1. Data Collection and Preprocessing: The first step is to gather relevant data sources, such as transaction logs, user activity logs, and historical fraud records. This data is then preprocessed to clean, transform, and normalize it for analysis.

```python
# Sample code for data preprocessing using Python and pandas
import pandas as pd

# Load data from source
transaction_data = pd.read_csv('transaction_logs.csv')

# Data cleaning and transformation
# (e.g., handling missing values, converting categorical variables)
```

2. Feature Engineering: Next, meaningful features are extracted from the preprocessed data to train the fraud detection model. Feature engineering involves selecting relevant attributes and creating new features that capture important characteristics of fraudulent behavior.

```python
# Sample code for feature engineering
# (e.g., calculating transaction frequency, average transaction amount)
transaction_data['transaction_frequency'] = transaction_data.groupby('user_id')['timestamp'].transform('count')
transaction_data['average_transaction_amount'] = transaction_data.groupby('user_id')['amount'].transform('mean')
```

3. Model Training: Machine learning models, such as logistic regression, random forests, or neural networks, are trained using the engineered features to predict the likelihood of fraud for each transaction or user.

```python
# Sample code for model training using scikit-learn
from sklearn.model_selection import train_test_split
from sklearn.ensemble import RandomForestClassifier
```

```
# Split data into training and testing sets
X_train, X_test, y_train, y_test = 
train_test_split(features, labels, test_size=0.2, 
random_state=42)

# Train Random Forest classifier
rf_classifier = RandomForestClassifier()
rf_classifier.fit(X_train, y_train)
```

4. Model Deployment: Once trained, the fraud detection model is deployed as a serverless function or microservice, allowing it to be invoked via API calls. Cloud providers like AWS Lambda or Google Cloud Functions offer seamless deployment of serverless applications.

```python
# Sample code for deploying model as a serverless function using AWS Lambda
import boto3

# Create Lambda client
lambda_client = boto3.client('lambda')

# Define function payload and invoke Lambda function
payload = {'transaction_data': transaction_data}
```

```
response = lambda_client.invoke(FunctionName='fraud_detection_function', Payload=json.dumps(payload))
```

5. Real-time Inference: Incoming transactions or user activities are sent to the deployed fraud detection function for real-time inference. The model evaluates each transaction and assigns a fraud score, which indicates the likelihood of fraudulent behavior.

```python
# Sample code for real-time inference
def detect_fraud(transaction_data):
    # Invoke fraud detection model
    response = lambda_client.invoke(FunctionName='fraud_detection_function', Payload=json.dumps(transaction_data))
    fraud_score = json.loads(response['Payload'].read())

    # Take appropriate action based on fraud score
    if fraud_score > threshold:
        # Flag transaction as potential fraud
        alert_fraud_team(transaction_data)
    else:
        # Process transaction normally
        process_transaction(transaction_data)
```

6. Continuous Monitoring and Improvement: The fraud detection system is continuously monitored to evaluate its performance and effectiveness. Any new data or fraudulent patterns are used to retrain the model periodically, ensuring that it remains adaptive to emerging threats.

```python
# Sample code for model retraining
def retrain_model(new_data):
    # Incorporate new data into training set
    updated_data = merge_data(old_data, new_data)

    # Retrain model with updated data
    updated_model = train_model(updated_data)

    return updated_model
```

Implementing a serverless fraud detection system powered by machine learning and AI technologies can significantly enhance a business's ability to detect and prevent fraudulent activities. By leveraging scalable infrastructure and advanced analytics, businesses can stay ahead of fraudsters and safeguard their operations, finances, and reputation. However, it's essential to continuously monitor and improve the system to adapt to evolving threats and ensure robust protection against fraud.

Predictive Analytics: Foreseeing the Future with AI Insights

Predictive analytics empowers businesses to anticipate future trends, behaviors, and outcomes by analyzing historical data and identifying patterns using machine learning and artificial intelligence (AI) techniques. In this comprehensive guide, we'll explore how organizations can harness the power of serverless machine learning and AI to gain valuable insights and make informed decisions about the future.

Introduction to Predictive Analytics

Predictive analytics is a branch of advanced analytics that utilizes historical data, statistical algorithms, and machine learning models to forecast future events or behaviors. By uncovering hidden patterns and relationships within data, predictive analytics enables organizations to make proactive decisions, mitigate risks, and capitalize on opportunities.

The Role of Machine Learning and AI in Predictive Analytics

Machine learning and AI play a crucial role in predictive analytics by automating the process of model building and enabling the discovery of complex patterns in large datasets. These technologies enable predictive models to continuously learn and improve over time, resulting in more accurate forecasts and insights.

Serverless Architecture for Scalable Predictive Analytics

Serverless architecture offers a scalable and cost-effective solution for implementing predictive analytics systems. By leveraging cloud-based serverless computing services, organizations can dynamically allocate resources based on demand, ensuring that predictive models can handle large volumes of data and scale seamlessly as the workload fluctuates.

Building a Serverless Predictive Analytics System

Let's outline the steps involved in building a serverless predictive analytics system using machine learning and AI:

1. Data Collection and Preparation: The first step is to gather relevant data sources, such as historical sales data, customer demographics, website traffic, or sensor readings. This data is then preprocessed to clean, transform, and normalize it for analysis.

```python
# Sample code for data preprocessing using Python and pandas
import pandas as pd

# Load data from source
sales_data = pd.read_csv('sales_data.csv')

# Data cleaning and transformation
# (e.g., handling missing values, converting categorical variables)
```

2. Feature Engineering: Next, meaningful features are extracted from the preprocessed data to train the predictive models. Feature engineering involves selecting relevant attributes and creating new features that capture important characteristics of the data.

```python
# Sample code for feature engineering
# (e.g., extracting time-based features, calculating aggregate statistics)
sales_data['month'] = pd.to_datetime(sales_data['date']).dt.month
```

```
sales_data['day_of_week'] =
pd.to_datetime(sales_data['date']).dt.dayofweek
```

3. Model Training: Machine learning models, such as linear regression, decision trees, or neural networks, are trained using the engineered features to predict future outcomes or behaviors.

```python
# Sample code for model training using scikit-learn
from sklearn.model_selection import train_test_split
from sklearn.linear_model import LinearRegression

# Split data into training and testing sets
X_train, X_test, y_train, y_test = train_test_split(features, labels, test_size=0.2, random_state=42)

# Train Linear Regression model
lr_model = LinearRegression()
lr_model.fit(X_train, y_train)
```

4. Model Deployment: Once trained, the predictive models are deployed as serverless functions or microservices, allowing them to be invoked via API calls. Cloud providers like AWS Lambda or Google

Cloud Functions offer seamless deployment of serverless applications.

```python
# Sample code for deploying model as a serverless function using AWS Lambda
import boto3

# Create Lambda client
lambda_client = boto3.client('lambda')

# Define function payload and invoke Lambda function
payload = {'sales_data': sales_data}
response = lambda_client.invoke(FunctionName='predictive_analytics_function', Payload=json.dumps(payload))
```

5. Real-time Predictions: Incoming data or events are sent to the deployed predictive analytics function for real-time predictions. The model evaluates the data and provides insights or forecasts, enabling organizations to make informed decisions quickly.

```python
# Sample code for real-time predictions
def predict_sales(sales_data):
    # Invoke predictive analytics model
```

```
    response = lambda_client.invoke(FunctionName='predictive_analytics_function', Payload=json.dumps(sales_data))
    sales_forecast = json.loads(response['Payload'].read())

    # Take appropriate action based on forecast
    if sales_forecast > threshold:
        # Allocate additional resources or inventory
        adjust_operations(sales_forecast)
    else:
        # Maintain current operations
        continue_operations()
```

6. Continuous Monitoring and Improvement: The predictive analytics system is continuously monitored to evaluate its performance and accuracy. Any new data or changes in patterns are used to retrain the models periodically, ensuring that they remain effective and relevant over time.

```python
# Sample code for model retraining
def retrain_models(new_data):
    # Incorporate new data into training set
    updated_data = merge_data(old_data, new_data)

    # Retrain models with updated data
```

updated_models = train_models(updated_data)

return updated_models
```

Predictive analytics powered by serverless machine learning and AI technologies enables organizations to gain valuable insights into future trends, behaviors, and outcomes. By leveraging scalable infrastructure and advanced analytics, businesses can make proactive decisions, mitigate risks, and capitalize on opportunities in a rapidly evolving landscape. However, it's essential to continuously monitor and improve predictive models to ensure their effectiveness and relevance over time.
```

Chapter 7

Training and Managing Your Serverless AI Models

Training Pipelines in the Serverless World

Training pipelines are the backbone of machine learning and artificial intelligence systems, enabling the seamless development, deployment, and management of models. In the serverless world, training pipelines offer scalability, flexibility, and cost-effectiveness, making them an ideal choice for building robust machine learning solutions. In this guide, we'll explore how organizations can leverage serverless technologies to implement training pipelines for machine learning and AI applications, complete with code examples.

<u>Introduction to Training Pipelines</u>

Training pipelines are workflows that orchestrate the process of training machine learning models, from data ingestion and preprocessing to model evaluation and deployment. These pipelines automate repetitive tasks, ensure consistency, and enable collaboration among data scientists, engineers, and other stakeholders.

<u>Benefits of Serverless Training Pipelines</u>

Serverless architecture offers several advantages for building training pipelines:

1. Scalability: Serverless computing platforms, such as AWS Lambda or Google Cloud Functions, automatically scale resources based on demand, allowing training pipelines to handle large volumes of data and compute-intensive tasks efficiently.

2. Flexibility: Serverless services enable developers to focus on building and deploying pipelines without managing infrastructure, making it easier to experiment with different algorithms, frameworks, and data sources.

3. Cost-effectiveness: With serverless computing, organizations only pay for the compute resources consumed during pipeline execution, eliminating the need to provision and maintain costly infrastructure.

Building a Serverless Training Pipeline

Let's outline the steps involved in building a serverless training pipeline for machine learning and AI applications:

1. Data Ingestion and Preprocessing: The first step is to ingest raw data from various sources, such as databases, data lakes, or streaming platforms. The data is then preprocessed to clean, transform, and prepare it for training.

```python
# Sample code for data ingestion and preprocessing using Python and pandas
import pandas as pd

# Load raw data from source
raw_data = pd.read_csv('raw_data.csv')

# Data cleaning and transformation
# (e.g., handling missing values, converting categorical variables)
```

2. Feature Engineering: Next, meaningful features are extracted from the preprocessed data to train the machine learning models. Feature engineering involves selecting relevant attributes and creating new features that capture important characteristics of the data.

```python
# Sample code for feature engineering
# (e.g., extracting time-based features, calculating aggregate statistics)
```

```
raw_data['month'] =
pd.to_datetime(raw_data['date']).dt.month
raw_data['day_of_week'] =
pd.to_datetime(raw_data['date']).dt.dayofweek
```

3. Model Training: Machine learning models, such as linear regression, decision trees, or neural networks, are trained using the engineered features to predict target variables or outcomes.

```python
# Sample code for model training using scikit-learn
from sklearn.model_selection import train_test_split
from sklearn.linear_model import LinearRegression

# Split data into training and testing sets
X_train, X_test, y_train, y_test = train_test_split(features, labels, test_size=0.2, random_state=42)

# Train Linear Regression model
lr_model = LinearRegression()
lr_model.fit(X_train, y_train)
```

4. Model Evaluation: Trained models are evaluated using performance metrics such as accuracy, precision, recall, or F1 score to assess their effectiveness in making predictions.

```python
# Sample code for model evaluation
from sklearn.metrics import accuracy_score

# Make predictions on test data
y_pred = lr_model.predict(X_test)

# Calculate accuracy score
accuracy = accuracy_score(y_test, y_pred)
print('Accuracy:', accuracy)
```

5. Model Deployment: Once trained and evaluated, models are deployed as serverless functions or microservices, allowing them to be invoked via API calls for inference or prediction.

```python
# Sample code for deploying model as a serverless function using AWS Lambda
import boto3

# Create Lambda client
lambda_client = boto3.client('lambda')
```

```
# Define function payload and invoke Lambda function
payload = {'model': lr_model, 'data': test_data}
response = lambda_client.invoke(FunctionName='prediction_function', Payload=json.dumps(payload))
```

6. Continuous Monitoring and Improvement: The training pipeline is continuously monitored to track model performance, identify issues, and incorporate feedback. Any new data or changes in patterns are used to retrain the models periodically, ensuring that they remain accurate and up-to-date.

```python
# Sample code for model retraining
def retrain_model(new_data):
    # Incorporate new data into training set
    updated_data = merge_data(old_data, new_data)

    # Retrain model with updated data
    updated_model = train_model(updated_data)

    return updated_model
```

Training pipelines are essential components of machine learning and AI systems, enabling organizations to develop, deploy, and manage models effectively. In the serverless world, training pipelines offer scalability, flexibility, and cost-effectiveness, making them an ideal choice for building robust machine learning solutions. By leveraging serverless technologies, organizations can streamline the development process, accelerate time-to-market, and achieve better outcomes with their machine learning initiatives.

Model Versioning and Control: Keeping Track of Your AI Evolution

Model versioning and control are critical aspects of managing machine learning and artificial intelligence (AI) models effectively. In the serverless world, where models are deployed as functions or microservices, it's essential to have robust versioning mechanisms in place to track changes, collaborate with team members, and ensure the reproducibility and reliability of models. In this guide, we'll explore how organizations can implement model versioning and control using serverless technologies, complete with code examples.

Introduction to Model Versioning and Control

Model versioning and control involve managing the lifecycle of machine learning and AI models, including versioning different iterations of models, tracking changes, and maintaining a history of experiments and results. This enables organizations to understand the evolution of models, reproduce experiments, and deploy models with confidence.

Challenges in Model Versioning in the Serverless World

In the serverless world, where models are deployed as functions or microservices, traditional versioning approaches may not be directly applicable. Challenges in model versioning in the serverless world include:

1. Scalability: Serverless architectures enable auto-scaling of resources, making it challenging to track and manage multiple versions of models deployed across distributed environments.

2. Dependency Management: Serverless functions often rely on external dependencies, such as libraries or frameworks, which may introduce compatibility issues when deploying different versions of models.

3. Collaboration: Collaborating on model development and experimentation requires mechanisms for sharing and versioning code, data, and configurations among team members.

Implementing Model Versioning and Control in the Serverless World

Let's outline the steps involved in implementing model versioning and control using serverless technologies:

1. Code Versioning with Git

Git is a widely-used version control system for tracking changes in code repositories. By using Git, organizations can manage different versions of model code, track changes, and collaborate with team members effectively.

```bash
# Initialize Git repository
git init

# Add model code files
git add .

# Commit changes
git commit -m "Initial commit"

# Create a new branch for feature development
git checkout -b feature-branch

# Make changes to model code
# (e.g., update model architecture, hyperparameters)
```

```
# Commit changes to feature branch
git commit -m "Update model architecture"

# Merge feature branch into main branch
git checkout main
git merge feature-branch
```

2. Data Versioning with DVC

Data Version Control (DVC) is an open-source version control system for managing data and models in machine learning projects. DVC allows organizations to track changes in data, collaborate on datasets, and reproduce experiments reliably.

```bash
# Install DVC
pip install dvc

# Initialize DVC repository
dvc init

# Add data files to DVC
dvc add data.csv

# Commit changes to DVC repository
```

```
dvc commit -m "Add data files"

# Push changes to remote repository
dvc push
```

3. Model Deployment with Serverless Functions

Serverless functions, such as AWS Lambda or Google Cloud Functions, enable organizations to deploy models as microservices that can be invoked via API calls. By versioning serverless function deployments, organizations can track changes in model configurations and environments.

```bash
# Deploy model as a serverless function using AWS Lambda
aws lambda create-function --function-name my-function --runtime python3.8 --handler lambda_function.lambda_handler --role role-arn --zip-file fileb://function.zip

# Update function code with new version
aws lambda update-function-code --function-name my-function --zip-file fileb://function.zip
```

4. Model Monitoring and Logging

Monitoring and logging are essential for tracking the performance and behavior of deployed models. By integrating monitoring and logging tools, organizations can capture metrics, logs, and alerts to detect anomalies and ensure the reliability of models in production.

```python
# Sample code for logging in Python
import logging

# Configure logging
logging.basicConfig(level=logging.INFO, format='%(asctime)s - %(levelname)s - %(message)s')

# Log model predictions
logging.info('Predictions: {}'.format(predictions))
```

5. Continuous Integration and Continuous Deployment (CI/CD)

CI/CD pipelines automate the process of building, testing, and deploying models, enabling organizations to iterate quickly and deploy changes to production with confidence.

```yaml
# Sample CI/CD pipeline configuration using GitHub Actions
name: CI/CD

on:
  push:
    branches:
      - main

jobs:
  build:
    runs-on: ubuntu-latest

    steps:
    - name: Checkout repository
      uses: actions/checkout@v2

    - name: Build and test model
      run: |
        # Add commands to build and test model code
```

Model versioning and control are essential for managing the lifecycle of machine learning and AI models effectively. In the serverless world, where models are deployed as functions or microservices, organizations must implement robust versioning mechanisms to track changes, collaborate with team members, and ensure the reproducibility and reliability of models. By leveraging serverless technologies and best practices for versioning and control, organizations can streamline model development, deployment, and management processes, ultimately delivering more reliable and scalable AI solutions.

Monitoring and Debugging Your Serverless AI Applications

Monitoring and debugging are crucial aspects of ensuring the reliability, performance, and efficiency of serverless AI applications. In the serverless world, where applications are composed of functions or microservices, monitoring and debugging tools play a vital role in detecting and diagnosing issues, optimizing resource utilization, and maintaining the health of deployed models. In this guide, we'll explore how organizations can effectively monitor and debug their serverless AI applications, complete with code examples.

Introduction to Monitoring and Debugging

Monitoring involves collecting, analyzing, and visualizing metrics, logs, and events generated by serverless AI applications. Debugging, on the other hand, is the process of identifying and resolving issues or errors in the application code, configuration, or infrastructure. Together, monitoring and debugging tools provide visibility into the performance and behavior of serverless AI applications, enabling organizations to detect, diagnose, and resolve issues quickly.

Challenges in Monitoring and Debugging Serverless AI Applications

In the serverless world, monitoring and debugging serverless AI applications pose several challenges:

1. Distributed Nature: Serverless applications are composed of multiple functions or microservices deployed across distributed environments, making it challenging to track and monitor the flow of data and events.

2. Cold Start Latency: Serverless functions experience cold start latency, where the first invocation of a function may incur additional latency due to provisioning and initialization of resources.

3. Resource Utilization: Optimizing resource utilization, such as memory and CPU, is essential for improving performance and reducing costs in serverless environments.

Implementing Monitoring and Debugging in Serverless AI Applications

Let's outline the steps involved in implementing monitoring and debugging for serverless AI applications:

1. Instrumentation and Logging

Instrumentation involves adding code to serverless functions to capture metrics, logs, and events. Logging frameworks, such as Python's logging module or CloudWatch Logs in AWS, enable developers to log information, errors, and debug messages generated by serverless functions.

```python
# Sample code for logging in Python using the logging module
import logging

# Configure logging
logging.basicConfig(level=logging.INFO, format='%(asctime)s - %(levelname)s - %(message)s')

# Log information
logging.info('This is an informational message')

# Log error
```

```
try:
    # Code that may raise an error
except Exception as e:
    logging.error('An error occurred: {}'.format(e))
```

2. Metric Collection and Visualization

Metric collection involves capturing performance metrics, such as invocation count, duration, and error rate, for serverless functions. Visualization tools, such as CloudWatch Metrics in AWS or Grafana, enable organizations to visualize and analyze metrics to gain insights into the behavior and performance of serverless AI applications.

```python
# Sample code for capturing custom metrics in Python using CloudWatch
import boto3

# Create CloudWatch client
cloudwatch = boto3.client('cloudwatch')

# Capture custom metric
cloudwatch.put_metric_data(
    Namespace='CustomMetrics',
    MetricData=[
```

```
{
    'MetricName': 'CustomMetric',
    'Value': 1,
    'Unit': 'Count',
    'Dimensions': [
        {
            'Name': 'FunctionName',
            'Value': 'my-function'
        }
    ]
```
```

## 3. Distributed Tracing

Distributed tracing involves tracking the flow of requests and events across distributed components of serverless AI applications. Tracing frameworks, such as AWS X-Ray or Jaeger, enable organizations to trace requests, identify bottlenecks, and diagnose issues in serverless applications.

```python
# Sample code for distributed tracing in Python using AWS X-Ray
from aws_xray_sdk.core import xray_recorder
from aws_xray_sdk.core import patch_all

# Patch all supported libraries for X-Ray tracing
patch_all()
```
```

```
# Define function handler
def lambda_handler(event, context):
    # Start tracing segment
    with xray_recorder.in_segment('MySegment'):
        # Function logic
```

4. Automated Alerts and Notifications

Automated alerts and notifications enable organizations to proactively detect and respond to issues or anomalies in serverless AI applications. CloudWatch Alarms in AWS or Prometheus Alertmanager can be configured to send alerts via email, SMS, or other communication channels based on predefined thresholds or conditions.

```yaml
# Sample CloudFormation template for creating a CloudWatch Alarm
Resources:
  MyAlarm:
    Type: AWS::CloudWatch::Alarm
    Properties:
      AlarmDescription: 'My Alarm'
      Namespace: AWS/Lambda
      MetricName: Errors
      Dimensions:
```

```
      - Name: FunctionName
        Value: 'my-function'
      Statistic: Sum
      Period: 60
      EvaluationPeriods: 1
      Threshold: 1
      ComparisonOperator: GreaterThanThreshold
```

5. Continuous Integration and Deployment (CI/CD)

CI/CD pipelines automate the process of building, testing, and deploying serverless AI applications, enabling organizations to iterate quickly and deploy changes to production with confidence. Integration with CI/CD tools, such as Jenkins or GitHub Actions, ensures that monitoring and debugging configurations are consistently applied across environments.

```yaml
# Sample GitHub Actions workflow for deploying serverless function
name: Deploy

on:
  push:
    branches:
      - main
```

```
jobs:
  deploy:
    runs-on: ubuntu-latest

    steps:
      - name: Checkout repository
        uses: actions/checkout@v2

      - name: Deploy serverless function
        run: |
          # Add commands to deploy serverless function
```

Monitoring and debugging are essential for ensuring the reliability, performance, and efficiency of serverless AI applications. In the serverless world, where applications are composed of functions or microservices, organizations must implement robust monitoring and debugging practices to detect, diagnose, and resolve issues quickly. By leveraging instrumentation, logging, metrics, tracing, alerts, and CI/CD pipelines, organizations can gain visibility into the behavior and performance of serverless AI applications, ultimately delivering more reliable and scalable solutions.

Chapter 8

Serverless Batch Processing: Handling Large Datasets with Ease

In today's data-driven world, organizations are dealing with increasingly large datasets. Analyzing these datasets efficiently is crucial for deriving valuable insights. Serverless batch processing offers a scalable and cost-effective solution for handling these large datasets. Leveraging serverless computing, machine learning, and artificial intelligence (AI), organizations can process data in batches without worrying about infrastructure management or scalability issues. In this article, we'll explore serverless batch processing in depth, along with practical examples and code snippets.

Understanding Serverless Batch Processing:
Serverless computing abstracts away infrastructure management, allowing developers to focus solely on writing code. With serverless batch processing, tasks such as data preprocessing, model training, and analysis can be executed without provisioning or managing servers. Cloud providers like AWS, Azure, and Google Cloud offer serverless platforms like AWS Lambda, Azure Functions, and Google Cloud Functions, which execute code in response to events or triggers.

Benefits of Serverless Batch Processing:

1. Scalability: Serverless platforms automatically scale resources based on workload demands, ensuring efficient processing of large datasets.

2. Cost-effectiveness: With serverless computing, organizations only pay for the resources consumed during execution, eliminating the need for provisioning and maintaining costly infrastructure.

3. Simplified Management: Developers can focus on writing code rather than managing servers, leading to increased productivity and faster time-to-market.

4. Fault Tolerance: Serverless platforms handle infrastructure failures gracefully, ensuring high availability and reliability of batch processing tasks.

Example Use Cases:

1. Image Processing: Batch process large collections of images for tasks such as object detection, image classification, or image enhancement.

2. Natural Language Processing (NLP): Analyze text data in batches for sentiment analysis, text summarization, or language translation.

3. Data Transformation: Perform ETL (Extract, Transform, Load) operations on large datasets to prepare them for analysis or machine learning.

4. Financial Data Analysis: Analyze financial data in batches for fraud detection, risk assessment, or predictive modeling.

5. IoT Data Processing: Process streams of sensor data collected from IoT devices for anomaly detection, predictive maintenance, or optimization.

Implementing Serverless Batch Processing: Let's dive into a practical example of implementing serverless batch processing using AWS Lambda and Python. In this example, we'll create a Lambda function to preprocess a large dataset of images for an image classification task.

```python
import boto3
import os
from PIL import Image
import numpy as np

# Initialize AWS SDK
s3 = boto3.client('s3')
```

```python
def preprocess_image(bucket_name, input_key, output_key):
    # Download image from S3
    input_path = '/tmp/input.jpg'
    s3.download_file(bucket_name, input_key, input_path)

    # Preprocess image
    img = Image.open(input_path)
    img = img.resize((224, 224))  # Resize image for model input
    img_array = np.array(img) / 255.0  # Normalize pixel values
    img_array = np.expand_dims(img_array, axis=0)  # Add batch dimension

    # Save preprocessed image to S3
    output_path = '/tmp/output.npy'
    np.save(output_path, img_array)
    s3.upload_file(output_path, bucket_name, output_key)

def lambda_handler(event, context):
    # Get bucket and key from event
    bucket_name = event['Records'][0]['s3']['bucket']['name']
    input_key = event['Records'][0]['s3']['object']['key']
```

```
    output_key = input_key.replace('input', 'output')  #
Change output key

    preprocess_image(bucket_name, input_key,
output_key)

    return {
        'statusCode': 200,
        'body': 'Image preprocessing complete'
    }
```

In this Lambda function:

- We download an image from an S3 bucket.

- Preprocess the image (resize and normalize pixel values).

- Save the preprocessed image back to the S3 bucket.

Serverless batch processing provides a flexible and efficient way to handle large datasets, leveraging the power of serverless computing, machine learning, and artificial intelligence. By abstracting away infrastructure management and scaling resources dynamically, organizations can focus on deriving insights from their data without worrying about infrastructure constraints. With the example provided and the wealth of services offered by cloud providers, organizations can harness the full potential of serverless batch processing to unlock valuable insights from their data.

Optimizing Performance and Cost Efficiency

As organizations increasingly adopt serverless computing, optimizing performance and cost efficiency becomes paramount, especially in machine learning (ML) and artificial intelligence (AI) workloads. While serverless architectures offer scalability and flexibility, inefficient resource utilization can lead to higher costs and slower processing times. In this article, we'll explore strategies for optimizing performance and cost efficiency in serverless ML and AI workflows, accompanied by practical examples and code snippets.

Understanding Performance and Cost Optimization in Serverless ML/AI: Optimizing performance and cost efficiency in serverless ML/AI involves balancing resource allocation, workload distribution, and infrastructure utilization. Key factors to consider include:

1. Resource Provisioning: Determining the appropriate amount of computational resources (e.g., memory, CPU) required for each task.

2. Parallelization: Distributing workloads across multiple concurrent executions to maximize resource utilization and reduce processing time.

3. Cold Start Optimization: Minimizing the latency associated with cold starts, where serverless functions are initialized for the first time.

4. Data Transfer Costs: Optimizing data transfer between services and minimizing inter-service communication overhead.

5. Monitoring and Optimization: Continuously monitoring resource usage, performance metrics, and costs to identify optimization opportunities.

<u>Example Use Cases:</u>

1. Image Classification: Optimize a serverless image classification pipeline to efficiently process large volumes of images while minimizing costs.

2. Natural Language Processing (NLP): Improve the performance and cost efficiency of serverless NLP tasks such as sentiment analysis or text summarization.

3. Model Inference: Optimize the deployment of serverless ML models for real-time inference with low latency and cost-effective resource utilization.

4. Data Preprocessing: Streamline data preprocessing pipelines to prepare large datasets for training or analysis efficiently.

5. Automated Model Training: Develop serverless workflows for automated model training and hyperparameter optimization with optimized resource utilization.

Optimizing Performance and Cost Efficiency with Serverless ML/AI: Let's explore optimization strategies with a practical example of optimizing a serverless image classification pipeline using AWS Lambda and Amazon S3.

```python
import boto3
import os
from PIL import Image
import numpy as np
import time

# Initialize AWS SDK
s3 = boto3.client('s3')
```

```python
def preprocess_image(bucket_name, input_key, output_key):
    # Download image from S3
    input_path = '/tmp/input.jpg'
    s3.download_file(bucket_name, input_key, input_path)

    # Preprocess image
    img = Image.open(input_path)
    img = img.resize((224, 224))  # Resize image for model input
    img_array = np.array(img) / 255.0  # Normalize pixel values
    img_array = np.expand_dims(img_array, axis=0)  # Add batch dimension

    # Save preprocessed image to S3
    output_path = '/tmp/output.npy'
    np.save(output_path, img_array)
    s3.upload_file(output_path, bucket_name, output_key)

def lambda_handler(event, context):
    start_time = time.time()

    # Get bucket and key from event
```

```
    bucket_name = event['Records'][0]['s3']['bucket']['name']
    input_key = event['Records'][0]['s3']['object']['key']
    output_key = input_key.replace('input', 'output')  # Change output key

    preprocess_image(bucket_name, input_key, output_key)

    end_time = time.time()
    execution_time = end_time - start_time
    print("Execution Time:", execution_time)

    return {
        'statusCode': 200,
        'body': 'Image preprocessing complete'
    }
```

Optimization Strategies:

1. Memory Allocation: Adjust the memory allocation for Lambda functions based on the memory requirements of the task to optimize performance and cost.

2. Parallel Execution: Trigger multiple Lambda functions concurrently to process multiple images in parallel, reducing overall processing time.

3. Reduce Cold Starts: Implement warm-up strategies such as scheduled executions or pre-warming Lambda functions to minimize cold start latency.

4. Efficient Data Transfer: Optimize data transfer between Lambda functions and S3 by minimizing redundant data transfers and leveraging efficient data formats.

5. Cost Monitoring: Continuously monitor Lambda usage, S3 storage costs, and data transfer costs using AWS Cost Explorer or similar tools to identify cost-saving opportunities.

Optimizing performance and cost efficiency in serverless ML/AI workflows requires a combination of resource optimization, workload distribution, and cost monitoring strategies. By implementing techniques such as memory allocation tuning, parallel execution, cold start optimization, efficient data transfer, and cost monitoring, organizations can maximize the value of serverless computing while minimizing costs and processing time. With the example provided and the wealth of services offered by cloud providers, organizations can achieve optimal performance and cost efficiency in their serverless ML/AI workflows, unlocking the full potential of their data-driven initiatives.

Security Considerations for Serverless AI Applications

As serverless computing continues to gain popularity, organizations are increasingly leveraging it for building and deploying AI applications. However, ensuring the security of serverless AI applications presents unique challenges and considerations. In this article, we'll explore key security considerations for serverless AI applications, along with practical strategies and code examples to mitigate potential risks.

Understanding Security Challenges in Serverless AI Applications: Serverless AI applications combine the complexities of AI and serverless computing, posing unique security challenges:

1. Data Privacy: AI applications often deal with sensitive data such as personal information or proprietary business data, raising concerns about data privacy and compliance with regulations like GDPR or HIPAA.

2. Model Security: AI models are valuable intellectual property and need to be protected against unauthorized access, tampering, or intellectual property theft.

3. Infrastructure Security: Serverless platforms abstract away infrastructure management, making it essential to ensure the security of underlying resources and prevent unauthorized access.

4. Injection Attacks: Serverless functions are susceptible to injection attacks, including SQL injection, code injection, and command injection, which can exploit vulnerabilities in function inputs or dependencies.

5. Denial of Service (DoS) Attacks: Malicious actors can target serverless applications with DoS attacks to disrupt service availability or exhaust resources, leading to downtime or performance degradation.

Security Considerations for Serverless AI Applications: Let's explore security considerations for serverless AI applications along with practical strategies and code examples to address each challenge.

1. Data Encryption: Encrypt sensitive data at rest and in transit to protect against unauthorized access. Leverage encryption libraries and services provided by cloud providers.

```python
# Example: Encrypting sensitive data with AWS Key Management Service (KMS)
import boto3

def encrypt_data(data):
    kms = boto3.client('kms')
    response = kms.encrypt(
        KeyId='your_kms_key_id',
        Plaintext=data
    )
    encrypted_data = response['CiphertextBlob']
    return encrypted_data
```

2. Access Control: Implement least privilege access control to restrict access to AI models, data storage, and other resources. Use IAM roles and policies to define fine-grained permissions.

```python
# Example: IAM policy to restrict access to specific S3 buckets
{
    "Version": "2012-10-17",
```

```
    "Statement": [
      {
        "Effect": "Allow",
        "Action": "s3:GetObject",
        "Resource": "arn:aws:s3:::your-bucket/*"
      },
        "Effect": "Deny",
        "Action": "s3:GetObject",
        "Resource": "arn:aws:s3:::your-bucket/sensitive-data/*",
        "Condition": {
          "StringNotEquals": {
            "aws:userid": [
              "your-allowed-user-id"
            
        }
```

3. Secure AI Model Deployment: Ensure secure deployment of AI models by implementing authentication, authorization, and encryption mechanisms. Use secure endpoints and protocols for model inference.

```python
# Example: Deploying a secure API endpoint for model inference using AWS API Gateway
import boto3
```

```python
def deploy_api_endpoint():
    api_gateway = boto3.client('apigateway')
    response = api_gateway.create_rest_api(
        name='secure-model-api'
    )
    api_id = response['id']
    # Create API resources, methods, and integration with Lambda function
    # Implement authentication and authorization mechanisms
    # Configure HTTPS endpoint
    return api_id
```

4. Injection Attack Prevention: Implement input validation, parameterized queries, and sanitization techniques to prevent injection attacks. Use security libraries and frameworks to mitigate injection vulnerabilities.

```python
# Example: Preventing SQL injection with parameterized queries in AWS Lambda
import boto3
import pymysql

def query_database(user_input):
```

```
    rds = boto3.client('rds')
    db_host = 'your-db-host'
    db_user = 'your-db-user'
    db_password = 'your-db-password'
    db_name = 'your-db-name'

    conn = pymysql.connect(host=db_host, user=db_user, password=db_password, database=db_name)
    cursor = conn.cursor()
    query = "SELECT * FROM users WHERE username=%s"
    cursor.execute(query, (user_input,))
    result = cursor.fetchall()
    conn.close()
    return result
```

5. DoS Mitigation: Implement rate limiting, request throttling, and monitoring/alerting mechanisms to detect and mitigate DoS attacks. Leverage cloud provider services for automatic scaling and resource isolation.

```python
# Example: Implementing request throttling in AWS API Gateway
import boto3

def configure_request_throttling(api_id):
```

```
    api_gateway = boto3.client('apigateway')
    response = api_gateway.update_usage_plan(
        usagePlanId='your-usage-plan-id',
        patchOperations=[
            {
                'op': 'replace',
                'path': '/throttle/rateLimit',
                'value': '1000'  # Set rate limit to 1000 requests per second
            }
        return response
```

Securing serverless AI applications requires a comprehensive approach encompassing data encryption, access control, model security, injection attack prevention, and DoS mitigation. By implementing security best practices, leveraging cloud provider security services, and staying vigilant against emerging threats, organizations can build and deploy serverless AI applications with confidence, ensuring the confidentiality, integrity, and availability of their AI-powered solutions. With the practical strategies and code examples provided, organizations can enhance the security posture of their serverless AI applications and mitigate potential security risks effectively.

Chapter 9

Emerging Trends and Advancements in Serverless Technologies

Serverless computing has revolutionized the way organizations build and deploy applications by abstracting away infrastructure management and allowing developers to focus on writing code. This paradigm shift has been particularly impactful in the fields of machine learning (ML) and artificial intelligence (AI), where scalable and cost-effective solutions are crucial. As serverless technologies continue to evolve, several emerging trends and advancements are shaping the future of serverless ML and AI. In this article, we will explore these trends and advancements, accompanied by practical examples and code snippets.

1. Advanced Orchestration with Serverless Functions

One of the key trends in serverless technologies is the advancement in orchestration capabilities. Modern serverless platforms now offer sophisticated tools to orchestrate complex workflows involving multiple functions. Services like AWS Step Functions, Azure Durable Functions, and Google Cloud Workflows enable developers to define and manage workflows that can handle complex branching, error handling, and retry logic.

Example: Orchestrating an ML Pipeline with AWS Step Functions

```python
import json
import boto3

# Define a simple Step Functions state machine for an ML pipeline
state_machine_definition = {
    "Comment": "A simple ML pipeline",
    "StartAt": "Preprocessing",
    "States": {
        "Preprocessing": {
            "Type": "Task",
            "Resource": "arn:aws:lambda:us-east-1:123456789012:function:PreprocessFunction",
            "Next": "ModelTraining"
        },
        "ModelTraining": {
            "Type": "Task",
            "Resource": "arn:aws:lambda:us-east-1:123456789012:function:TrainModelFunction",
            "Next": "ModelEvaluation"
        },
```

```
        "ModelEvaluation": {
            "Type": "Task",
            "Resource": "arn:aws:lambda:us-east-1:123456789012:function:EvaluateModelFunction",
            "End": True
        }
# Create the state machine
client = boto3.client('stepfunctions')
response = client.create_state_machine(
    name='MLPipelineStateMachine',
    definition=json.dumps(state_machine_definition),
    roleArn='arn:aws:iam::123456789012:role/service-role/StepFunctionsMLRole'
)

print(response['stateMachineArn'])
```
```

## 2. Serverless Machine Learning Model Serving

Model serving has traditionally been a challenge in deploying ML models at scale. Serverless technologies are addressing this by providing managed services that simplify the deployment and scaling of ML models. Services like AWS SageMaker, Azure Machine Learning, and Google AI Platform now offer serverless endpoints for deploying and serving ML models.
```

Example: Deploying a Model with AWS SageMaker Serverless Inference

```python
import boto3

# Create a SageMaker model
sagemaker_client = boto3.client('sagemaker')
model_name = 'my-model'
model_data_url = 's3://my-bucket/path/to/model.tar.gz'

create_model_response = sagemaker_client.create_model(
    ModelName=model_name,
    PrimaryContainer={
        'Image': '123456789012.dkr.ecr.us-east-1.amazonaws.com/my-sagemaker-image:latest',
        'ModelDataUrl': model_data_url
    },
    ExecutionRoleArn='arn:aws:iam::123456789012:role/SageMakerExecutionRole'
)

# Create a serverless endpoint configuration
endpoint_config_name = 'my-endpoint-config'
```

```
create_endpoint_config_response =
sagemaker_client.create_endpoint_config(
    EndpointConfigName=endpoint_config_name,
    ProductionVariants=[
        {
            'VariantName': 'AllTraffic',
            'ModelName': model_name,
            'ServerlessConfig': {
                'MemorySizeInMB': 2048,
                'MaxConcurrency': 5
            }
        }
# Deploy the serverless endpoint
endpoint_name = 'my-serverless-endpoint'
create_endpoint_response =
sagemaker_client.create_endpoint(
    EndpointName=endpoint_name,
    EndpointConfigName=endpoint_config_name
)

print(f"Endpoint {endpoint_name} is being created.")
```
```

## 3. Event-Driven Data Processing

Event-driven architectures are becoming increasingly popular in serverless computing, allowing applications to respond in real-time to events such as data changes, user actions, or system events. This is particularly useful for
```

data processing pipelines, where serverless functions can be triggered by events from data streams, message queues, or file uploads.

Example: Real-Time Data Processing with AWS Lambda and Kinesis

```python
import boto3

# Create a Kinesis stream
kinesis_client = boto3.client('kinesis')
stream_name = 'my-data-stream'
kinesis_client.create_stream(
    StreamName=stream_name,
    ShardCount=1
)

# Define a Lambda function to process data from the Kinesis stream
lambda_client = boto3.client('lambda')
lambda_function_code = """
import json

def lambda_handler(event, context):
    for record in event['Records']:
        payload = record['kinesis']['data']
        print(f"Decoded payload: {json.loads(payload)}")
```

"""

```
lambda_client.create_function(
    FunctionName='ProcessKinesisDataFunction',
    Runtime='python3.8',
    Role='arn:aws:iam::123456789012:role/lambda-execution-role',
    Handler='index.lambda_handler',
    Code={
        'ZipFile': bytes(lambda_function_code, 'utf-8')
    }
# Create an event source mapping to trigger the Lambda function
# when records are added to the Kinesis stream
lambda_client.create_event_source_mapping(
    EventSourceArn=f'arn:aws:kinesis:us-east-1:123456789012:stream/{stream_name}',
    FunctionName='ProcessKinesisDataFunction',
    StartingPosition='LATEST'
)

print(f"Lambda function ProcessKinesisDataFunction is set up to process records from Kinesis stream {stream_name}.")
```
```

## 4. Enhanced Security and Compliance
```

As serverless applications handle increasingly sensitive data, security and compliance are paramount. Emerging serverless technologies are incorporating advanced security features, including enhanced identity and access management, encryption, and automated compliance checks. Serverless security tools now offer capabilities such as automatic vulnerability scanning, anomaly detection, and policy enforcement.

Example: Implementing AWS Lambda Security with IAM and Encryption

```python
import boto3

# Define an IAM policy for the Lambda function
policy_document = {
    "Version": "2012-10-17",
    "Statement": [
        {
            "Effect": "Allow",
            "Action": [
                "s3:GetObject",
                "s3:PutObject"
            ],
            "Resource": "arn:aws:s3:::my-secure-bucket/*"
        }
    ]
}
iam_client = boto3.client('iam')
```

```python
policy_response = iam_client.create_policy(
    PolicyName='LambdaS3AccessPolicy',
    PolicyDocument=json.dumps(policy_document)
)

policy_arn = policy_response['Policy']['Arn']

# Create a Lambda execution role and attach the policy
role_response = iam_client.create_role(
    RoleName='LambdaExecutionRole',
    AssumeRolePolicyDocument=json.dumps({
        "Version": "2012-10-17",
        "Statement": [
            {
                "Effect": "Allow",
                "Principal": {
                    "Service": "lambda.amazonaws.com"
                },
                "Action": "sts:AssumeRole"
            }
        ]
iam_client.attach_role_policy(
    RoleName='LambdaExecutionRole',
    PolicyArn=policy_arn
)

# Create the Lambda function with encryption
lambda_client = boto3.client('lambda')
lambda_function_code = """
```

```python
import boto3
import base64
from botocore.exceptions import ClientError

def lambda_handler(event, context):
    s3 = boto3.client('s3')
    bucket_name = 'my-secure-bucket'
    object_key = 'my-encrypted-data'

    # Encrypt data
    kms_client = boto3.client('kms')
    plaintext_data = b'My secret data'
    encrypted_data = kms_client.encrypt(
        KeyId='your-kms-key-id',
        Plaintext=plaintext_data
    )['CiphertextBlob']

    # Upload encrypted data to S3
    s3.put_object(
        Bucket=bucket_name,
        Key=object_key,
        Body=encrypted_data
    )

    return {
        'statusCode': 200,
        'body': 'Data encrypted and uploaded to S3'
    }
```

```
lambda_client.create_function(
    FunctionName='SecureDataProcessingFunction',
    Runtime='python3.8',
    Role=role_response['Role']['Arn'],
    Handler='index.lambda_handler',
    Code={
        'ZipFile': bytes(lambda_function_code, 'utf-8')
    }
print(f"Lambda function SecureDataProcessingFunction created with enhanced security.")
```

5. AI-Powered Serverless Management

The integration of AI and serverless technologies is leading to the development of AI-powered management tools. These tools use machine learning algorithms to optimize resource allocation, predict traffic patterns, and automatically adjust configurations for optimal performance and cost efficiency. AI-driven insights can also help in identifying security vulnerabilities and performance bottlenecks.

Example: Using AWS Lambda Power Tuning for Optimizing Performance

AWS Lambda Power Tuning is an open-source tool that helps you optimize the memory configuration of your

Lambda functions. It uses a step function to run multiple configurations and selects the optimal one.

```python
import boto3

# Define a Step Functions state machine for Lambda Power Tuning
state_machine_definition = {
   "Comment": "AWS Lambda Power Tuning",
   "StartAt": "Initialize",
   "States": {
     "Initialize": {
        "Type": "Pass",
        "Next": "InvokeLambda"
     },
```

```python
     "InvokeLambda": {
        "Type": "Task",
        "Resource": "arn:aws:lambda:us-east-1:123456789012:function:YourLambdaFunction",
        "Parameters": {
           "Payload": {
              "input": "test"
           }
        },
        "Next": "AnalyzePerformance"
     },
```

```
    "AnalyzePerformance": {
      "Type": "Pass",
      "ResultPath": "$.result",
      "Next": "EndState"
    },
    "EndState": {
      "Type": "Succeed"
    }
# Create the state machine
client = boto3.client('stepfunctions')
response = client.create_state_machine(
   name='LambdaPowerTuningStateMachine',
   definition=json.dumps(state_machine_definition),
   roleArn='arn:aws:iam::123456789012:role/service-role/StepFunctionsExecutionRole'
)

print(response['stateMachineArn'])
```

6. Serverless Edge Computing

Edge computing is an emerging trend that involves processing data closer to where it is generated, reducing latency and bandwidth usage. Serverless edge computing extends the benefits of serverless to edge locations, enabling real-time processing and analytics at the edge. Services like AWS Lambda@Edge and Cloudflare

Workers allow developers to run serverless functions at edge locations, providing low-latency responses and improved performance for end users.

Example: Running a Serverless Function at the Edge with AWS Lambda@Edge

```python
import boto3

# Create a Lambda function for edge processing
lambda_client = boto3.client('lambda')
lambda_function_code = """
def lambda_handler(event, context):
    request = event['Records'][0]['cf']['request']
    headers = request['headers']

    # Add a custom header to the request
    headers['x-custom-header'] = [{'key': 'X-Custom-Header', 'value': 'my-value'}]

    return request
"""

lambda_client.create_function(
    FunctionName='EdgeProcessingFunction',
    Runtime='python3.8',
```

```
    Role='arn:aws:iam::123456789012:role/lambda-edge-execution-role',
    Handler='index.lambda_handler',
    Code={
        'ZipFile': bytes(lambda_function_code, 'utf-8')
    }
# Associate the function with a CloudFront distribution
client = boto3.client('cloudfront')
distribution_id = 'your-distribution-id'
response = client.update_distribution(
    Id=distribution_id,
    DistributionConfig={
        # existing distribution configuration
        'DefaultCacheBehavior': {
            'LambdaFunctionAssociations': {
                'Quantity': 1,
                'Items': [
                    {
                        'LambdaFunctionARN': 'arn:aws:lambda:us-east-1:123456789012:function:EdgeProcessingFunction:1',
                        'EventType': 'viewer-request'
                    }
```
print(f"Lambda function EdgeProcessingFunction associated with CloudFront distribution {distribution_id}.")
```
```

7. AutoML and Serverless

Automated machine learning (AutoML) is another trend making waves in the serverless domain. AutoML frameworks simplify the process of training and tuning machine learning models by automating tasks such as feature selection, hyperparameter tuning, and model selection. Serverless AutoML solutions, like Google Cloud AutoML, AWS SageMaker Autopilot, and Azure AutoML, provide scalable and cost-effective ways to build high-quality models without requiring extensive ML expertise.

Example: Using AWS SageMaker Autopilot for AutoML

```python
import boto3

sagemaker_client = boto3.client('sagemaker')

# Define the input data for the AutoML job
input_data_config = [
    {
        'DataSource': {
            'S3DataSource': {
                'S3DataType': 'S3Prefix',
                'S3Uri': 's3://your-bucket/path/to/training-data/'
```

```
    }
    'TargetAttributeName': 'target'
}
# Define the output data configuration
output_data_config = {
    'S3OutputPath': 's3://your-bucket/path/to/output-data/'
}

# Create an AutoML job
response = sagemaker_client.create_auto_ml_job(
    AutoMLJobName='automl-job',
    InputDataConfig=input_data_config,
    OutputDataConfig=output_data_config,
    ProblemType='BinaryClassification',
    AutoMLJobObjective={
        'MetricName': 'Accuracy'
    },

RoleArn='arn:aws:iam::123456789012:role/SageMakerExecutionRole'
)

print(f"AutoML job created with name: {response['AutoMLJobArn']}")
```

The serverless computing landscape is rapidly evolving, bringing about significant advancements and new trends that are transforming how organizations build and deploy AI applications. From advanced orchestration capabilities and serverless model serving to real-time event-driven processing, enhanced security measures, AI-powered management tools, edge computing, and AutoML, serverless technologies are becoming more powerful and versatile.

These emerging trends not only simplify the development and deployment of machine learning and AI applications but also enhance their performance, scalability, and security. By leveraging these advancements, organizations can unlock new possibilities, driving innovation and gaining a competitive edge in their respective industries.

As serverless technologies continue to evolve, staying abreast of these trends and adopting best practices will be crucial for developers and organizations aiming to harness the full potential of serverless computing for their AI and ML workloads. The examples and code snippets provided in this article offer a glimpse into how these emerging trends can be implemented in practice, paving the way for more efficient, secure, and scalable serverless AI applications.

The Ethical Implications of AI and Serverless Development

The rapid advancement of artificial intelligence (AI) and serverless development technologies has revolutionized the tech landscape, offering unprecedented capabilities and efficiencies. However, these advancements also bring forth a host of ethical concerns that need to be addressed to ensure the responsible and fair deployment of these technologies. This essay explores the ethical implications of AI and serverless development, particularly in the context of serverless machine learning and AI applications.

Understanding AI and Serverless Development

Artificial Intelligence (AI) refers to the simulation of human intelligence in machines designed to think and learn like humans. These systems use algorithms and vast amounts of data to recognize patterns, make decisions, and predict outcomes. Machine Learning (ML), a subset of AI, involves training models on data to perform tasks such as classification, regression, and clustering.

Serverless Development is a cloud computing model that abstracts server management. Developers can run code in response to events without provisioning or managing servers. Functions-as-a-Service (FaaS), such as AWS Lambda, and Backend-as-a-Service (BaaS), like Firebase, are prime examples. Serverless architecture enhances scalability and reduces operational overhead, allowing developers to focus on writing code.

Combining serverless architecture with AI/ML offers numerous advantages, including cost efficiency, scalability, and rapid deployment. However, this convergence also amplifies ethical concerns, which we will explore through several lenses.

Ethical Implications in AI and Serverless Development

1. Data Privacy and Security

AI systems often require large datasets to function effectively. These datasets can include sensitive personal information, raising significant privacy concerns. In a serverless environment, data is stored and processed in the cloud, which adds another layer of complexity to data security.

Example: Consider a serverless AI application that processes user health data to provide personalized fitness recommendations. The following AWS Lambda function demonstrates how user data might be processed:

```python
import json
import boto3

def lambda_handler(event, context):
    user_data = json.loads(event['body'])
    # Process user data for fitness recommendations
    recommendations = generate_recommendations(user_data)

    return {
        'statusCode': 200,
        'body': json.dumps(recommendations)
    }

def generate_recommendations(data):
    # Placeholder for AI/ML model inference
    # Assume model is loaded and predictions are made
    return {"recommendation": "Exercise 30 minutes daily"}
```

In this example, sensitive user data is processed by the AI model. Ensuring that this data is securely transmitted, stored, and handled is crucial to maintaining user trust and complying with data protection regulations such as GDPR or CCPA.

2. Bias and Fairness

AI systems can perpetuate and even amplify biases present in training data. In a serverless setup, the rapid deployment of AI models can lead to widespread dissemination of biased systems before biases are detected and mitigated.

Example: An AI recruitment tool deployed on a serverless architecture might inadvertently favor candidates from certain demographics if the training data is not representative.

```python
import json
import boto3

def lambda_handler(event, context):
    candidate_data = json.loads(event['body'])
    # Assess candidate using AI model
    assessment = assess_candidate(candidate_data)

    return {
        'statusCode': 200,
        'body': json.dumps(assessment)
    }
```

```
def assess_candidate(data):
    # Placeholder for AI/ML model inference
    # Assume model is loaded and assessments are made
    return {"assessment": "Strong Candidate"}
```

In this scenario, ethical AI practices dictate the need for diverse and representative training datasets and continuous monitoring to detect and correct biases.

3. Transparency and Accountability

Serverless AI systems can operate with minimal human intervention, which raises questions about accountability and transparency. Users and stakeholders should be able to understand how decisions are made by AI systems.

Example: A financial application that uses a serverless AI system to approve loans must ensure that the decision-making process is transparent.

```python
import json
import boto3

def lambda_handler(event, context):
    application_data = json.loads(event['body'])
    # Evaluate loan application using AI model
```

```
    decision = evaluate_loan(application_data)

    return {
      'statusCode': 200,
      'body': json.dumps(decision)
    }

def evaluate_loan(data):
    # Placeholder for AI/ML model inference
    # Assume model is loaded and decisions are made
    return {"decision": "Approved"}
```

Transparency can be achieved by logging the decision-making process and providing explanations for decisions, which can be audited and reviewed.

4. Environmental Impact

Serverless computing is often perceived as more environmentally friendly due to its efficient resource utilization. However, the underlying infrastructure still requires significant energy, especially for AI model training and inference.

Example: Training large AI models in a serverless environment can lead to substantial energy consumption. Developers should consider the environmental footprint and strive to use energy-efficient algorithms and cloud services powered by renewable energy.

```python
import json
import boto3

def lambda_handler(event, context):
    training_data = json.loads(event['body'])
    # Train AI model
    model = train_model(training_data)

    return {
        'statusCode': 200,
        'body': json.dumps({"status": "Model Trained"})
    }

def train_model(data):
    # Placeholder for model training logic
    # Assume model is trained with data
    return {"model": "Trained Model"}
```

Organizations can also offset their carbon footprint by investing in renewable energy projects or purchasing carbon credits.

5. Job Displacement and Economic Impact

AI and serverless technologies can lead to job displacement as automation replaces manual tasks. While these technologies can create new opportunities, they also require a workforce with new skill sets.

Example: A serverless AI system that automates customer service inquiries might reduce the need for human operators.

```python
import json
import boto3

def lambda_handler(event, context):
    inquiry_data = json.loads(event['body'])
    # Process inquiry using AI model
    response = process_inquiry(inquiry_data)

    return {
        'statusCode': 200,
        'body': json.dumps(response)
    }

def process_inquiry(data):
    # Placeholder for AI/ML model inference
    # Assume model processes inquiry and generates response
```

```
    return {"response": "Your issue has been resolved"}
```

Organizations should consider the broader economic impact and invest in reskilling and upskilling programs to help workers transition to new roles.

Addressing Ethical Implications

To address these ethical implications, stakeholders must adopt a multi-faceted approach:

1. Regulation and Governance: Governments and regulatory bodies need to establish clear guidelines and frameworks for AI and serverless development. These regulations should ensure data privacy, mitigate biases, and promote transparency.

2. Ethical AI Practices: Developers and organizations should adhere to ethical AI principles, such as fairness, accountability, and transparency. This includes using diverse datasets, providing clear explanations for AI decisions, and regularly auditing AI systems for biases and errors.

3. Stakeholder Engagement: Engaging with stakeholders, including users, employees, and communities, can provide valuable insights into the ethical implications of AI and serverless technologies. This engagement can help identify potential issues early and develop solutions that are fair and equitable.

4. Sustainability Initiatives: Organizations should prioritize sustainability by adopting energy-efficient technologies, reducing their carbon footprint, and supporting renewable energy initiatives.

5. Education and Reskilling: Investing in education and reskilling programs is crucial to preparing the workforce for the changes brought about by AI and serverless technologies. This includes providing training in new skills and supporting career transitions.

The ethical implications of AI and serverless development are profound and multifaceted. While these technologies offer significant benefits, they also pose challenges that require careful consideration and proactive measures. By prioritizing ethical practices, engaging stakeholders, and investing in sustainable and equitable solutions, we can harness the power of AI and serverless development to create a better future for all.

Chapter 10

Your Journey to Serverless AI Mastery: The Final Call to Action

Embarking on the journey to master serverless AI has been a transformative experience. Along the way, you've learned to harness the power of cutting-edge technologies, from serverless architectures to sophisticated machine learning models. This journey has equipped you with the skills to build scalable, efficient, and cost-effective AI solutions. Now, it is time to channel this knowledge into real-world applications that can drive positive change. Let's recap the critical milestones of this journey and explore how you can unleash the power of AI for good.

The Foundations of Serverless AI

<u>Understanding Serverless Architecture</u>

Serverless architecture revolutionized the way we think about deploying and managing applications. By abstracting away the underlying infrastructure, serverless allows developers to focus on writing code and building functionality without worrying about server management. In the context of AI, this means deploying machine learning models and AI services with ease, scalability, and cost-efficiency.

Key components of serverless architecture include:

1. AWS Lambda: A compute service that runs code in response to events and automatically manages the compute resources required by that code.

2. Amazon S3: A scalable object storage service for storing data, including datasets used for training machine learning models.

3. AWS API Gateway: A service for creating, deploying, and managing secure APIs at any scale.

4. AWS SageMaker: A fully managed service that provides every developer and data scientist with the ability to build, train, and deploy machine learning models quickly.

Building and Deploying Machine Learning Models

The journey began with understanding the basics of machine learning and progressing to building complex models. Using AWS SageMaker, you learned how to streamline the entire machine learning lifecycle:

1. **Data Preparation:** Utilizing Amazon S3 to store and preprocess data.

2. **Model Training:** Leveraging SageMaker's built-in algorithms or custom models for training.

3. **Model Deployment:** Deploying trained models using SageMaker endpoints or through Lambda functions for serverless inference.

Here is an example of deploying a trained model using AWS Lambda:

```python
import json
import boto3

sagemaker = boto3.client('sagemaker-runtime')

def lambda_handler(event, context):
    data = json.loads(event['body'])
    response = sagemaker.invoke_endpoint(
        EndpointName='your-sagemaker-endpoint',
        Body=json.dumps(data),
        ContentType='application/json'
    )
    result = json.loads(response['Body'].read().decode())
    return {
```

```
    'statusCode': 200,
    'body': json.dumps(result)
}
```

Real-Time Inference and API Integration

A significant part of your journey was learning to integrate AI models into applications that can provide real-time inference. Using AWS Lambda in conjunction with API Gateway, you created serverless APIs that can process requests, invoke machine learning models, and return predictions in real time.

Here is an example of creating a serverless API using AWS API Gateway and Lambda:

1. Define API in API Gateway: Create a new API and configure methods (e.g., POST) to invoke the Lambda function.

2. Integrate Lambda Function: Link the Lambda function that performs model inference.

3. Test the API: Deploy the API and test it using tools like Postman or curl.

Advanced Topics and Best Practices

Security and Compliance

As you progressed, ensuring the security and compliance of your AI solutions became paramount. Implementing best practices such as:

1. IAM Roles and Policies: Defining precise permissions for Lambda functions and SageMaker services.

2. Encryption: Encrypting data at rest and in transit using AWS KMS.

3. Monitoring and Logging: Using AWS CloudWatch for monitoring, logging, and alerting.

Optimization and Cost Management

Optimizing the performance and cost of your serverless AI solutions involved:

1. Right-Sizing Resources: Choosing the appropriate instance types and configurations for training and inference.

2. Auto-Scaling: Leveraging SageMaker's auto-scaling capabilities to handle varying workloads.

3. Cost Analysis: Regularly reviewing cost reports and utilizing AWS Budgets to keep expenses in check.

Unleashing the Power of AI for Good

Now that you have mastered serverless AI, it is time to put your skills to use for the greater good. AI has immense potential to address some of the world's most pressing challenges. Here are a few areas where you can make a significant impact:

Healthcare

AI can revolutionize healthcare by improving diagnosis, treatment, and patient care. For example, you can develop a serverless AI solution to analyze medical images for early detection of diseases.

```python
import boto3
import numpy as np
from PIL import Image

# Load the model (assuming it's stored in S3)
s3 = boto3.client('s3')
model_bucket = 'your-model-bucket'
model_key = 'model/path/to/your/model.h5'
```

```python
# Download and load the model
s3.download_file(model_bucket, model_key, '/tmp/model.h5')
model = load_model('/tmp/model.h5')

def lambda_handler(event, context):
    # Preprocess the image
    image_data = event['body']
    image = Image.open(io.BytesIO(base64.b64decode(image_data)))
    image = image.resize((224, 224))
    image_array = np.array(image) / 255.0
    image_array = np.expand_dims(image_array, axis=0)

    # Predict
    prediction = model.predict(image_array)
    result = {'prediction': prediction.tolist()}

    return {
        'statusCode': 200,
        'body': json.dumps(result)
    }
```

Environmental Monitoring

AI can help monitor and protect the environment. For instance, you can create a serverless AI application to analyze satellite images for deforestation and track changes over time.

```python
import boto3
import numpy as np
from skimage import io

def lambda_handler(event, context):
    # Load the satellite image from S3
    bucket = event['bucket']
    key = event['key']
    s3 = boto3.client('s3')
    s3.download_file(bucket, key, '/tmp/image.tif')

    # Analyze the image (e.g., using a pre-trained model for deforestation)
    image = io.imread('/tmp/image.tif')
    prediction = analyze_image(image)  # Replace with actual analysis logic

    return {
        'statusCode': 200,
        'body': json.dumps({'prediction': prediction})
    }
```

```
def analyze_image(image):
    # Placeholder for image analysis logic
    # Example: returning a dummy prediction
    return {'deforestation': np.random.rand()}
```

Education

AI can enhance educational outcomes by providing personalized learning experiences. You can build a serverless AI system to recommend tailored learning resources based on student performance.

```python
import boto3
import json

# Assuming a trained recommendation model
def lambda_handler(event, context):
    # Get student data from the event
    student_data = json.loads(event['body'])

    # Load the recommendation model (e.g., from S3)
    model = load_recommendation_model()

    # Generate recommendations
    recommendations = model.recommend(student_data)
```

```
    return {
        'statusCode': 200,
        'body': json.dumps({'recommendations': recommendations})
    }

def load_recommendation_model():
    # Placeholder for loading a recommendation model
    # Example: returning a dummy model
    class DummyModel:
        def recommend(self, data):
            return ['resource1', 'resource2', 'resource3']
    return DummyModel()
```

The Final Call to Action

Your journey to mastering serverless AI has equipped you with the knowledge and tools to build impactful solutions. Now, it is time to take action. Here are some steps to get started:

1. Identify a Problem: Choose a cause you are passionate about, whether it's healthcare, environmental conservation, education, or another area where AI can make a difference.

2. Prototype Your Solution: Leverage your serverless AI skills to develop a prototype. Start small, focusing on a specific problem and iteratively improve your solution.

3. Collaborate and Share: Partner with organizations, share your knowledge, and collaborate with others to enhance your solution's impact.

4. Deploy and Iterate: Deploy your solution using serverless infrastructure to ensure scalability and cost-efficiency. Continuously gather feedback and iterate to improve its effectiveness.

Mastering serverless AI is not just about acquiring technical skills; it's about applying those skills to create meaningful change. As you move forward, remember that the power of AI lies in its ability to amplify human potential and address complex challenges. By unleashing the power of AI for good, you can contribute to a better, more equitable world. The journey doesn't end here—it's just the beginning. Embrace the challenge, and let your innovations make a lasting impact.

Appendix

Glossary of Key Terms

Glossary of Key Terms in Serverless Machine Learning and Artificial Intelligence

1. Serverless Computing

Serverless computing is a cloud-computing execution model where the cloud provider dynamically manages the allocation and provisioning of servers. In this model, developers can build and run applications and services without worrying about server management. The serverless model allows for automatic scaling, and users are only charged for the compute resources they consume.

2. Function as a Service (FaaS)

FaaS is a category of cloud computing services that provides a platform allowing customers to develop, run, and manage application functionalities without the complexity of building and maintaining the infrastructure typically associated with developing and launching an app. FaaS is a key component of serverless architectures, enabling event-driven execution of functions.

3. Machine Learning (ML)

Machine Learning is a subset of artificial intelligence (AI) that involves the use of algorithms and statistical models to enable computers to improve their performance on a specific task through experience and data. ML applications are used in various domains, such as predictive analytics, natural language processing, and computer vision.

4. Artificial Intelligence (AI)

Artificial Intelligence refers to the simulation of human intelligence in machines that are programmed to think and learn like humans. AI systems can perform tasks that typically require human intelligence, such as visual perception, speech recognition, decision-making, and language translation.

5. Model Training

Model training is the process of teaching a machine learning algorithm to make predictions or take actions based on data. During training, the algorithm processes input data and adjusts its parameters to minimize errors. This involves iterating through data, optimizing the model's performance using techniques like gradient descent.

6. Inference

Inference in the context of machine learning refers to the process of using a trained model to make predictions on new, unseen data. Inference typically happens after the model has been deployed and is used to generate outputs for new inputs.

7. AutoML (Automated Machine Learning)

AutoML refers to the process of automating the end-to-end process of applying machine learning to real-world problems. AutoML solutions cover various stages, including data preprocessing, feature selection, model selection, hyperparameter tuning, and deployment, making ML accessible to users without extensive expertise in the field.

8. Event-Driven Architecture

Event-driven architecture (EDA) is a software architecture pattern promoting the production, detection, consumption of, and reaction to events. In serverless computing, EDA is common because serverless functions can be triggered by various events such as changes in data, user actions, or messages from other systems.

9. Cloud-Native

Cloud-native refers to applications designed and built to run on cloud infrastructure. These applications are optimized for scalability, flexibility, and resilience, leveraging cloud services such as serverless computing, container orchestration, and managed databases.

10. Microservices

Microservices are an architectural style that structures an application as a collection of loosely coupled services, each implementing a specific business capability. In the context of serverless computing, microservices can be deployed as independent serverless functions, which communicate with each other through APIs.

11. Containers

Containers are a lightweight, portable, and efficient way to encapsulate an application along with its dependencies, ensuring consistency across multiple environments. Technologies like Docker and Kubernetes are commonly used for managing containers in cloud-native and serverless environments.

12. API Gateway

An API Gateway is a server that acts as an API front-end, receiving API requests, enforcing throttling and security policies, passing requests to the back-end service, and then returning the appropriate response. In serverless architectures, API Gateways are often used to manage and route traffic to serverless functions.

13. Edge Computing

Edge computing is a distributed computing paradigm that brings computation and data storage closer to the location where it is needed to improve response times and save bandwidth. In AI and ML, edge computing allows for real-time data processing and inference at the source of data generation, such as IoT devices.

14. Orchestration

Orchestration refers to the automated arrangement, coordination, and management of complex computing environments and services. In serverless and microservices architectures, orchestration tools like AWS Step Functions or Kubernetes manage the execution of various services and functions.

15. Data Pipeline

A data pipeline is a series of data processing steps. Data is ingested from various sources, processed, and then stored or used for further analysis. In serverless ML, data pipelines automate the flow of data through different stages, from raw data to model training and deployment.

These terms encapsulate the foundational concepts of serverless machine learning and artificial intelligence, providing a solid basis for understanding the interplay between cloud computing, ML, and AI.

www.ingramcontent.com/pod-product-compliance
Lightning Source LLC
Chambersburg PA
CBHW031616210526
45464CB00004B/1599